PIMCO

A Brief History of the World's Biggest Bond Fund

Joan Oleck

**asset
international**

Business Intelligence for the World's Leading Financial Institutions

Published by:
Asset International, Inc.
805 Third Avenue
New York, NY 10022

Oleck, Joan
PIMCO:A Brief History of the World's Biggest Bond Fund

SKU# AIP104
Print ISBN 978-1-937504-88-5
eBook ISBN 978-1-937504-89-2

www.assetinternational.com

2014

"The Beach" Feels the Heat

The Pacific Investment Management Company, better known as Pimco, and even better known for it's ranking as the world's largest bond fund, is known on The Street as "The Beach." The reason: the firm's Newport Beach, California, headquarters' proximity to the blue waters of the Pacific.

But at The Beach on February 25, 2014, those blue waters were churning. In point of fact, a full-blown tsunami had struck.

A front-page story in the *Wall Street Journal* that day, headlined "Inside the Showdown at the World's Biggest Bond Firm," detailed internal conflicts that Pimco would have preferred stay quiet. The combatants: Pimco founder and managing director Bill Gross, long nicknamed the Bond King for his legendary expertise at trading bonds, not just holding them, and his number-two and heir-apparent, CEO Mohamed El-Erian.

Apparently there was no love lost between the two multi-millionaire executives.

"I have a 41-year track record of investing excellence," Gross had earlier told El-Erian, according to two witnesses' accounts at the *WSJ*. "What do you have?"

El-Erian's reply, according to the *Journal*: "I'm tired of cleaning up your s___."

The CEO's reference was to Gross's peculiarly rigid style of interacting with employees, but more on that below. There were other, more important, riptides forming among those Pacific waves. Indeed, El-Erian had shocked The Street by announcing his resignation in January (he would actually leave in March). Yet, what executive voluntarily leaves the world's largest bond firm, with $1.9 trillion (as of the first quarter of 2014) in assets under management?

An unhappy one, that's who. First, there were the factors outside El-Erian's control: Bonds were in a sorry state in general and traders everywhere, not just at Pimco, were feeling pressure. That pressure was reflected at the firm's leading fund, Pimco's Total Return Fund, which had produced 6.8 percent annualized returns for 14 years, but instead lost 1.9 percent in 2013, its first negative return in recent memory. Jittery investors, running for the exits, withdrew a reported net $41.1 billion that year.

Second, Gross's rigid management style wasn't doing anything to calm his troops. The lengthy *WSJ* article, which jumped inside from the home page for another six columns, detailed stories from multiple sources of Gross forbidding employees from speaking to him directly or making eye contact "especially in the morning" (giving new meaning to the term "morning person"). The managing director also handed out something called "communication demerits" for such trader offenses as neglecting to number the pages in a presentation. Those demerits, tracked by an assistant, could dampen year-end bonuses, the *Journal*'s Gregory Zuckerman reported.

Third on the list of possible reasons for El-Erian's unhappiness was the overall working environment at Pimco. This is a a workplace where most employees arrive at 4:30 a.m. (Pacific Time), fully two hours before the NYSE in New York rings the opening bell. Employees then stay until 5 p.m. (PST)—a 12.5-hour day that would have most shop stewards calling for a strike vote.

Add to these factors the discord between the two principals—El-Erian's comment about "cleaning up your ____" went directly to his disapproval of how Gross treated the staff—and you had the makings of his abrupt resignation. After the confrontation, Gross reportedly backed down a few notches, promising his CEO he would lessen his autocratic style, but whatever he actually did on that score was apparently not enough.

He had already—before the February 25 *WSJ* piece—denied that conflicts with El-Erian were a factor in the CEO's departure. "It had nothing to do with friction," Gross told the paper in an earlier interview. "Sometimes people will say, 'Gross is too challenging,' and maybe so. I would say [that] if you think I'm challenging now, you should have seen me 20 years ago."

Once the February 25 story was pending, and Gross knew El-Erian was leaving, he went into even stronger damage-control mode. A new management team of six, headed by former COO—now CEO Douglas Hodge—seemed designed to counter the autocracy claims. Describing what he called "superior results" for clients, Gross wrote in a prepared statement, "I ask of others only what I demand of myself: hard work, dedication, and intense focus on putting our clients first."

After the *WSJ* article broke, Gross defended himself yet again: "All this discourse about an autocratic style from my standpoint and conflict between Mohamed and myself is overblown," Gross said on the CNN show "Street Signs."

From Gross's standpoint, El-Erian opted to leave "because he told us he wasn't the man to implement his plan." And the characterizations about his refusal to talk to staff? "It was very, very unfair," he responded, in the CNN interview. El-Erian "had always been a good friend," he added of his CEO, describing socializing between their families, and a friendship between their wives.

★★★★★

The public didn't buy it. Through the 12 months ended that February, investors withdrew nearly $48 billion in investments, equating to more than half the money removed from all intermediate-term bond bonds, according to Morningstar Research. What's more, dating back to the previous October, the Pimco Total Return fund that Bill Gross managed had lost its crown as the world's largest mutual fund.

Then, on March 18, Morningstar downgraded Pimco's "stewardship" grade from B to C and cited reports that Gross had "a severe and reputed retaliatory temperament." In a kind of piling-on, the *New York Times* on March 23 ran a story headlined, "Tremors in the Palace of the Bond-Fund King," quoting a former Pimco senior executive, William

Powers. Powers confirmed the stories about the managing director, calling Gross "an autocrat" and noting, "Those who disagree do so at their peril." Regardless of this stinging criticism, Morningstar added later that week that Gross's fund remained "one of the best in the business." The *Times* similarly quoted Laird R. Landman, co-director of income at TCW, and a former Pimco staffer, as saying, "Bill Gross is a genius, the best there is at bond trading."

But the damage was done. "Many" institutional investors were reviewing their alliance with Pimco, the *New York Times* reported, and one of them, the Florida Retirement System Pension Plan, actually put the firm on a watch list. The nation's largest public pension fund, Calpers (California Public Employees Retirement System), meanwhile, confirmed it was "monitoring" the dissension at Pimco.

Financial commentators began murmuring, and not in a nice way, about how Pimco's 2013 performance had been subpar—a loss, though a small one, of 1.92 percent.

The commentary dwelled on how the Federal Reserve's decision to start cutting back its safety net for monetary policy in 2012 had hurt both Pimco as a whole and Gross's own Pimco Total Return

Fund. Gross had guessed—wrongly—that the Fed would not tighten monetary policy. In fact, the Fed had cut back its bond buying.

Forbes, the *Financial Times*, and Reuters all weighed in. Reuters columnist, Felix Salomon, actually raised the "R" word. "It's time for Bill Gross to retire," his column in February 2014 was headlined. Added Salomon: "Gross is old, he's erratic, and he's generally not someone you want to park your money with on the quasi-permanent time horizon which is used by Pimco clients like sovereign wealth funds and foundations."

In April, Reuters reported that top investors were pressing Pimco's parent, German asset management and insurance company, Allianz SE to "step up oversight;" one was even considering the unusual step of going public with its concerns during a shareholder meeting in May. Three major shareholders who shared their concerns with Reuters said they wanted Allianz to reexamine the new management structure put into place following El-Erian's exit—with six deputy investment officers under Gross. Investors large and small were getting nervous about Gross's freedom and his reported $200 million a year in pay as well as that 1.9 percent loss to Pimco's flagship Total Return Fund,—its worst performance since 1994—followed in the first three months of 2014 by an outflow of $15.45 billion from its U.S. open-end mutual funds.

In short, Gross's reputation was tainted, perhaps irretrievably. Would the soon-to-be 70-year-old (as of April 2014) leave of his own volition? Would he be pushed out? Those were questions on Wall Streeters' lips. As for the Bond King himself, he may well have been asking himself, "How did I get here?"

Chapter One

The 1970s

From Blackjack to Bonds

William Hunt Gross acquired his taste for risk early, right out of college in fact, and long before he ever read his first bond prospectus: Just barely into his twenties, he became expert at. . . blackjack.

But that's getting ahead of the story. Born on April 13, 1944, in Middletown, Ohio, to a steel company sales executive, Sewell "Dutch" Gross, and his wife Shirley, young Bill had a standard middle class upbringing. It was a big event, however, when the family moved to San Francisco. Young Bill was only ten years old when he set down roots in the Golden State. Yet even as he enjoyed the West Coast, when it came time for college, he, like many kids, wanted to put some distance between himself and home. So he chose Duke University in North Carolina, a basketball school with a vaunted academic reputation, he also chose to major in psychology. But that's where the "standard" part of his life veers off course.

During a car ride to pick up doughnuts for his
fraternity, Gross was severely injured when his car
smashed into oncoming traffic, propelling him
through the windshield. Three-quarters of his
scalp was cut off, which was horrible enough, but
things could have been much worse had not a state
trooper miraculously found and hand-carried the
scalp to the emergency room—a lucky break for the
college senior, who would spend most of that year
recovering in the hospital.

It was during his convalescence that Gross developed his interest in gambling, which one source
says he had been introduced to during a spring
break in the Bahamas (where he lost $100). While
in healing mode from the auto injuries, Gross filled
many of those dull hours poring through author Ed
Thorpe's book, *Beat the Dealer,* schooling himself
in Thorpe's system for counting cards, a means of
beating the house at blackjack.

During the summer of 1965, Gross had taken his
first real foray into that world, working at Harrah's
Casino in Lake Tahoe, Nevada, as a $5-per-hour
slot machine attendant. "Something about those
casinos attracted me early on," Gross later told
Canada's *The National Post.* To save money, he
said, he slept in his car, bathed in the famous
mountain lake and shaved at a Shell gas station.

Looking toward graduation in 1966, he enlisted in
the Navy, since the odds of being drafted for the
Vietnam war in those days were high and he hoped
to control his choices. But before he reported for
active duty, Gross wanted to test his self-education
in counting cards.

So, after graduating from Duke that May of 1966,
he headed to Sin City—Las Vegas this time—with
a mere $200 in his pocket. In Vegas, he checked
into the $6-per-night Indian Hotel on the Strip.
Then he hit the blackjack tables.

As Gross told Timothy Middleton, author of *The
Bond King* (John Wiley, 2004), he proceeded to
spend 16 hours a day playing blackjack. "I had no
friends. I had no girlfriend. I didn't go to the mov-
ies. I didn't stop to eat except at the buffets. It was
a compulsion to prove that the system worked,"
Gross said of that time in his life. Over the course
of four months he was rewarded for his efforts—
and his risk—with $10,000 in winnings.

He applied his winnings to graduate school, to
pursue an MBA. But first there was military
duty to get through, and while Gross had long
envisioned himself as a Navy pilot (think: *Top
Gun*), he discovered that he actually hated flying. So, he still wound up in Vietnam as did
most enlistees at the time. But instead of flying,

he remained earthbound, escorting Navy SEALS up jungle rivers to carry out dangerous secret missions. He survived; some of the SEALS he accompanied did not.

Returning safely stateside in 1969, Gross enrolled at UCLA's Anderson School of Management where he quickly identified his passion for all things stock market. His new passion proved to be an easy segue from blackjack into the business world.

As he later related to *The Globe and Mail*, he told himself at the time, "I obviously enjoy mathematical application of a system of some sort, and hard work and diligence. 'What's the adult form of gambling? It's the stock market. Maybe you can't outfox it, but let's see if it can be done.' Right then and there I said, 'I'm getting into the money management business.'"

His MBA topic, convertible bonds, helped him complete his degree in 1971, and subsequently land a job as a junior credit analyst (starting salary: $10,000) at the Pacific Mutual Life Insurance Company in Newport Beach. There, his first task was to clip bond coupons for investors, so they could receive their interest payments. Though Gross had hoped for what he considered a sexier job in equities, fate intervened. As Middleton pointed out in *The Bond King*, "He had landed at exactly the right place at exactly the right time."

★★★★★

Contrary to popular belief, Gross didn't found Pimco; it already existed before he came on the scene. Pac Mutual had founded an investment subsidiary, Pacific Investment Management Company (PIMCO, or Pimco, for short), in line with advice from McKinsey & Co., pursue equity mutual funds. The company was keen to take that advice; after all, it already had legions of insurance salespeople. So, why not put them to work selling something new? Pimco was incorporated in 1971 in Newport Beach.

A management team was needed, and Gross, who only recently had arrived, was quickly tapped. Completing what the company called its management "troika" were Bill Podlich and James Muzzy. Podlich had been first on the scene, taking a job as a credit analyst in private placements with Pac Mutual as early as 1966. Muzzy was hired at the same time as Gross. Both became portfolio managers. (Ott Thompson, who would become CEO, had been with Pac Mutual since 1968.)

Famously, the "troika," at Gross's urging, introduced the notion of diverging into fixed income— *actively managed* bond portfolios. Gross was trying

out techniques of active bond management, and
the results were positive. The insurance side of the
aisle wasn't enthusiastic. "After a year and a half,"
Muzzy told Middleton, "[the parent company]
discovered the insurance agents didn't want to get
close to mutual funds."

Yet, because Gross's immediate boss, Benjamin
Ehlert, liked the idea of active bond management,
and because standard bond management practices
were going nowhere fast, the investment committee
at Pac Mutual said yes to letting Ehlert run a $15
million in-house account. Ehlert then passed the
job on to Gross. And Walter Gerken, who at the
time headed Pac Mutual's investments (and would
become its chairman), approved; Gerken liked
Gross.

There was good reason: Postwar inflation was intense; banks were eager for new finance products;
bonds' lack of controls helped lower their price.
And Gross, unlike his bond-manager predecessors,
was eager to trade them. As the *Globe and Mail*
profile noted, "Rather than simply hold bonds, Mr.
Gross pioneered ways to trade them, generating fat
profits. He employs complex mathematical tools
but excels at making big-picture assessments of
economies, markets and governments, which then
direct his bets."

"It was still the age of carbon paper, typing pools, and expensive long distance calls," Middleton's book added, "when the most comprehensive data about bonds was published in a newspaper, the *Bond Buyer*. Bloomberg terminals were still a decade off. So Gross relied on what today seem primitive methods: telephone calls, for instance. Trading by phone, Gross might buy several millions of dollars worth of private placements (bought and sold only by institutions) and immediately sell his purchase, scoring a healthy profit."

Along the way, Gross had big ambitions. Two years after he started at Pimco, his parents visited and, as he related to the *Globe and Mail*, he confidently informed them he was going to be the best bond manager in the world. "Of course, they looked at me and said, 'What's that?' " he recalled, laughing.

Around this time he also met the number-one investor on the planet, Warren Buffett. Neither Gross nor Buffett had yet made his mark, but both were on the way up. Gross was a junior analyst; Buffett and his partner, Charlie Munger (vice chairman of Berkshire Hathaway), visited Pacific Mutual Life seeking to borrow $10 million to acquire the small company that would grow into the giant, GEICO. A team recommended the deal; Gross was on that team. He and Buffett would keep track of each other in subsequent years, and become mutual fans.

But, back to the 1970s. The decade brought a lot of changes to America as Pimco's website (pimco.com) points out: the opening of NASDAQ, the abandoning of the gold standard, the oil crisis. And changes were stirring at Pac Mutual, as well.

By 1973, Pimco's management troika had pioneered a tripartite management style. Muzzy took charge of explaining the firm's bond trading techniques to clients and keeping them happy; he had that kind of personality. Gross's style was more shy and close-mouthed; he stayed with the technical side of the business. Podlich, who was already assistant to Gerken, headed Pac Mutual's investments division; he was comfortable dealing with Pimco's administration and the business end of things. When Gerken became CEO, Podlich retained his role for the new investment leader, Ott Thompson.

Thus arose what the three began calling their "three-legged stool" leadership, comprising portfolio management (Gross), client servicing (Muzzy), and business administration (Podlich). The three men, the company website says, were in accord about running a lean and efficient operation, with flat management and no corner offices.

Middleton explained how the three-legged stool functioned as a business model: "Investment managers who worked for Gross have counterparts called account managers, who work for Muzzy," Middleton wrote. "The account teams are fully qualified to run portfolios, and switching between the two sides is not without precedent." It was the account teams, however, who communicated with the institutional clients that then, and now, comprise the lion's share of Pimco's Fortune 100 clients.

Apparently the three-part approach worked, as did Gross's active management of bonds, a relatively new idea at the time: In 1974, Pimco gained its first client, Southern California Edison Co. By the mid-1970s, the company website says, Pimco had $50 million under management, and, in 1976 or 1977 (sources differ), it acquired its first Fortune 500 client, AT&T—a major boost for the firm's credibility.

Another stroke of fortune occurred at about that same time. Its name was ERISA, the Employee Retirement Income Security Act, and one of its tenets was that pension fund managers function as fiduciaries, meaning they must act in their clients' best interest. This meant that these managers' actions must benefit the retirees, present and future, invested in the pension fund; they could not personally own large blocks of company stock nor do anything with that stock to benefit themselves.

In short, outside pension managers were now de rigueur, and Pimco was poised to market itself as a leader in the management of bonds, which in turn comprised the category of securities used in pension funds. This fact undoubtedly helped raise Pimco's assets under management, by 1981, to $2 billion.

Another sea change would occur, but not for some years into the future—1985, specifically—when Pimco formally became independent of Pacific Mutual. This separation had long been tacit, if not official. The insurance side was a tad staid, the investment side fiery and dynamic. And the two sides clearly weren't drinking chums. As Middleton tells it, there was—and here he quotes A. Michael Lipper, founder of the well-known mutual fund analysis company—"the parking lot problem."

Lipper described a scenario where the head of Pac Mutual would pull into his spot every day in his trusty Buick while the head of the investment unit arrived in his Ferrari. In short, there was tension over, um, compensation. And, what's more, the investment guys had leverage: Both they and their employer knew that, awaiting those young hotshots were plenty of greener pastures elsewhere.

★★★★★

A word should be added about exactly how Gross achieved his impressive turnaround of the slow, conservative world of bonds, using his "Total Return" method. This is the method that lay behind what, in the late 1980s, became formalized as the Total Return Fund. The particulars of this method are detailed in Middleton's book, as well as in Gross's own tome, *Bill Gross on Investing* (John Wiley & Sons, March 1998, first published as *Everything You've Heard About Investing Is Wrong: How to Profit in Coming Post-Bull Markets* (Times Books, 1997).

But a few salient points should be made. In 1971, when Gross came on the scene, Middleton wrote, "the typical professional bond investor (such as a bank trust officer) looked at bond returns the same way a widow or orphan would—generated by interest only." Bonds were issued at par, at one hundred cents for each dollar of face amount; and they were then held until maturity, ten to 30 years. Coupons attached to the bonds were clipped every six months and mailed to the issuer for that half year's interest payment. At maturity, 100 cents was returned.

Gross based his decisions, Middleton relates, on both *secular* and *cyclical* considerations. The first positions the core portfolio in a way that's least resistant to long-term (three to five years) trends in the geo economy and society. The resulting *secular analysis* relies on experts' identification of trends.

An example, says the author, is the aging of the U.S. population (happening even faster in Europe): Gross early on increased his holdings in companies in medical care and pharmaceuticals, which serve the aging population, as he sought ways to lessen the credit risks of bond issuers whose paper he held.

Cyclical trends, meanwhile, are changes affecting the market over shorter periods, like every quarter or even every day. The federal funds rate and investor edginess over political disruptions—say, the current pro-Russian insurgency in Ukraine, or the civil war in Syria—are examples. A related reaction by Gross was his entry into Treasury bonds in 2000 when he decided that stocks were overpriced and the economy was headed in a downward direction. This was followed by his reaction to 2003's rate rise. Pimco early on began selling Treasurys even as those T-notes' yield jumped (because bonds move inversely with yield).

Pimco also dumped home mortgage bonds, thinking that if aging boomers meant fewer home mortgages in subsequent years, mortgage bond prices would rise. Dumping doesn't make sense in that context, but Pimco's thinking was that companies like the government agencies Fannie Mae and Freddie Mac would be negatively affected if mortgage demand lessened. They would issue fewer mortgage bonds, letting the prices of previously issued bonds rise and those of newly issued bonds fall.

The two lessons from this, Middleton wrote, were: (1) that the perspectives of the stock investor and the bond investor are diametrically opposite; and (2) that while bond holders dread the Federal Reserve's expected post-recession move to raise interest rates now that the economy is doing better, those investors can still make their currently held bonds more valuable during economic dips and downturns.

Gross's background in gambling figured in here, Middleton wrote; he noted how Gross told him how those long-ago lessons at blackjack became the basis for the three main takeaways of his investing techniques. Takeway #1 was the notion of spreading risk. Pimco describes itself as an "investor for all seasons," meaning that Gross believes in investing even when the odds are not ideal. He's not some wild-eyed gambler here, Middleton noted, describing Pimco's "phalanx of computer jockeys" who constantly monitor market risks. This because of takeaway #2: Know the risks that exist and analyze and predict their impact.

Still, Gross did and does place big bets at times. (Takeaway #3: When the odds favor you, the best bet is a big one.) Gross, for instance, believes in putting 10 percent of a portfolio on a favored stock rather than spreading it among 50 stocks. "If you've got 10 mutual funds, you're too diversified," he wrote in his own book.

Above all, Gross believes in studying secular demographic trends. In what direction might those many baby boomers now coming of age take the economy? How much money will they withdraw from savings in their old age? What are the labor unions doing in Europe? And what about deflation? What impact will the powerhouse economies of China and India have?

Above all, now, in 2014, what will Gross et al. do about the seemingly endless bear market for bonds?

Chapter Two

The 1980s

Fame and Fortune: Part 1

The 1980s was the decade when Pimco came into its own, climbing out of obscurity (for non-institutional investors, at least) with a series of successes. For starters, its assets under management soared from $1 billion to $25 billion.

Those were the years of Reagonomics (which Bill Gross fervently supported), the Latin American debt crisis, and the rise of the "Tiger" economies. The 1980s also, infamously, was the decade of Black Monday, in October 1987, which brought economic turmoil to the markets.

But for Pimco, things were cooking. In 1980 it had its spinoff from Pac Mutual, staying a wholly owned subsidiary, but becoming an independent operating company with its own offices. In 1982, Pac Mutual also agreed to give Gross, Muzzy, and Podlich a share of the profits that their growing operation was creating. The move made the troika

wealthy men (although Pimco's subsequent acquisition as a subsidiary of Allianz, in 2000, would
make them even wealthier). Also benefiting were
the firm's two principals, Dean Meiling and Chris
Dialynas, whom Gross heavily relied on. Dialynas
would become managing director in 1987. Together, the five men called themselves the "partners."

A milestone during the partners' rise to fame and
fortune was Gross's debut, in 1981, of his much-
read "Investment Outlook" newsletter, which he
peppers with metaphors, poetry, and bits of folksy
wisdom (a sample from that first September edi-
tion: "Today's financial economy and markets are
making an extended visit to the dentist's office.")

The following year, 1982, saw the formal launch
of Pimco's influential "secular" view, in the form
of "secular forums"—annual retreats (for insiders
only) designed to help the firm establish a context
for financial decisions. These were high-profile
meetings which attracted the likes of popstar
speakers like Ben Bernanke, Zbigniew Brzezinski,
and Robert Reich.

Other highlights of the 1980s saw Gross's rise
as a regular on CNN and, starting in late 1985,
a panelist on Louis Rukeyser's popular PBS
show, *Wall Street Week*. Then there was Pimco's
1987 expansion into global fixed income and

currency investments, constituting, as the company website described it, a "broad array of international opportunities."

Also in 1987 came the introduction of a line of mutual funds based on Gross's Total Returns Strategy—the first in a suite of mutual funds.

One event that helped make the Total Return Fund hot was a lucky break early on, in 1981: Then-Federal Reserve chief Paul Volcker moved to bring down interest rates which, because of their inverse relationship with bonds, forced the latter's price to soar, bringing nice profits and sizable coupons to Pimco investors.

In 1986, Pimco's success won the seal of approval from *Institutional Investor* magazine, which that January headlined its lengthy feature "The PIMCO powerhouse," essentially a valentine to the firm. Sample: "With its deft blend of cautious timing and aggressive bets, Pacific Investment Management has beaten the pants off its fixed-income competitors."

Writer Diane Hal Gropper described Pimco's chief competitors at the time as Trust Co. of the West, Criterion Investment Management Co., Jennison Associates, and Miller, Anderson & Sherrerd. She wrote that, for the ten and five years ended December 1984, Pimco had beaten both the Salomon

Brothers and Shearson Lehman Brothers bond indexes, with compound annual returns of 11.8 percent and 13.5 percent, respectively. Pimco's performance won its first- and sixth-percentile scores in SEI Corp's bond manager rankings for those periods. In the 15 years leading up to that point, Gropper wrote, Pimco had yet to have a down year.

"PIMCO stands out on other counts as well," *Institutional Investor* opined. "Clients commend it for the attention it pays to service and communication. It has weathered both time and success with little turnover"—a reference to Gross's, Muzzy's, and Podlich's tenure from the firm's start. "Exceptionally creative and entrepreneurial," the publication said of Pimco's investment choices.

According to Gropper, by 1986, Pimco boasted a roster of 80 clients, including foundations and public and union pension funds, and 49 corporations, including GTE, Amoco, Chevron, 3M, Boeing, TRW, and Pfizer.

Like Middleton, in *The Bond King*, Gropper detailed Gross's philosophy. Her description included: 1) Look to the long term (paying less attention to housing starts and weekly money supply numbers than to, say, monetary policy); 2) Avoid extreme durations (Pimco takes the middle ground with maturities, creating portfolios of two-and-a-half to six years' time periods; this policy cost investors during bull markets but appealed to pension managers, Gropper wrote, who distrusted market-timing ventures of bonds and equities.

Next on the list was: 3) Bet on sectors, being ready to put up to 40 percent of a portfolio into one area, especially if those sectors are adjudged to be undervalued; and emphasize yield. Here, Gropper described Pimco's heavy reliance on mortgage pass-through securities, which, she wrote, had accounted for 40 percent of the firm's total portfolio. Last on the list was: 4) Stay on the cutting edge (figuring out innovative investment strategies and pleasing clients)—"They've got a good brain trust," Gropper wrote, quoting a Chevron manager of analysis. "They're always carefully searching for inefficiencies in the market, looking where others don't and finding them first."

Gropper gave high marks to the way Pimco devoted 10 percent of its portfolio to high coupon corporates that were callable within two years. Despite long maturities, such bonds traded like one- to two-year rates because of short call time spans— and they were cheap; so they substituted nicely for short-term Treasury notes. More praise went to futures and options, where Pimco had special expertise. As early as 1981 the firm had hedged a client's portfolio, and by the time the Department of Labor declared such activities free of ERISA violation, Pimco was way out ahead of other firms—though the pension funds in its client base were more than nervous about such investments.

Pimco demonstrated its ability to be out in front again in 1983, with a Ginnie Mae collateralized depository receipt futures contract: The firm spotted a contract provision offering a choice between a long position and short one. Pimco figured it couldn't lose and dropped $2 billion into the contracts, selling them a year later for a cool 2 percent profit. The firm later went on to play municipal bond futures and Treasury bond futures.

Finally, Gropper praised Pimco to the skies for its client-serving acumen—singling out its account managers in particular for their investment backgrounds and their practice of working with clients full-time, in contrast to other firms, which simply let portfolio managers do the job. "Clients say its quarterly reports are exceptionally well written. . . and give it high marks for the seminars it frequently holds on its investment strategy," the *Institutional Investor* article added.

Also singled out: Pimco's strategy to consolidate clients' mortgage-backed securities holdings into one fund handled by one bank, assuring on-time interest payments. Podlich won special praise for this part of the operation. "Podlich makes sure the business is run like a business," a portfolio manager named Closson Vaughan told Gropper.

Otherwise, *Institutional Investor* praised what it called Pimco's "open and entrepreneurial working environment" that—at least at that time— "encourages young people to participate," with a physical setup that eschewed corner offices in favor of meeting spaces. "There's tension and competitiveness to find new opportunities," Vaughan told the magazine. "Ninety-nine percent of the time it's handled in a kidding, good-natured way that keeps the environment relaxed and informal."

Of course that was back in 1986; the partners were still young and idealistic and weren't in charge of an investment fund that was anywhere near its multi-billion dollar size today.

★★★★★

Pimco had phenomenal growth during the 1980s. In late 1983, Frank Russell Trust Co. put Pimco on its roster of money managers, at the same time that its consulting arm began recommending the firm to its pension clients. Russell alone brought Pimco $800 million; and within two years (1985) the firm's assets exceeded $9 billion.

But then there was that *other* news headline from the financial sphere: Black Monday. On October 19,

1987, stock markets—starting with Hong Kong and moving west to Europe, then the United States—crashed, plummeting in value. The Dow Jones Industrial Average dropped 508 points, to 1738.

Just before that, in August, the *New York Times* had reported the prices of Treasury bonds falling, sharply raising yields to their highest levels that year. The pressure to sell had been caused by the dollar weakening against foreign currencies and signs of the Federal Reserve tightening monetary policy—though no one really knew what the new Fed chairman Alan Greenspan, who'd replaced Paul Volcker that July, would do. Whatever the cause, Treasury's 8 7/8 percent issue due in 2017 fell nearly 1 1/2 points, raising its yield to about 9.12 percent.

"The market has the same nervousness about the dollar as earlier this year, but now the widespread evidence of economic strength the past few months is an additional reason for expecting that bond yields will stay at these levels or move higher," Gross told the *Times*. He expressed the view that the economy was not susceptible to a downturn for several quarters, owing to a jobs gain, a drop in unemployment initial claims, a high level of consumer confidence, and growth in industrial production.

But then Black Monday occurred, and a year later, in various interviews in October 1988, Gross's tone turned considerably more hesitant: Pimco's managing director had just been chosen, in a survey of 100 money managers by *Pension & Investment Age*, as the man they, his peers, would most like to have managing their own portfolios. But Gross was not in a celebratory mood. Like other well-heeled portfolio managers, he was uncertain about interest rates and not about to commit funds. "We have $500 million that is ready to go to work," he told the *New York Times*. "But the odds favor a move to higher rates. Long rates would have to move back 9 1/8 percent to 9 1/4 percent before we would put that money to work."

In an interview with the *Los Angeles Times*, Gross warned about the trade deficit. "It's just a question of time," he said. "Our world trading partners only have so much tolerance in terms of the debt we owe." To balance the deficit, he said, might well lead to a lower dollar and higher inflation—with a bond market correction and lower stock prices. Or the alternative might be measures to prompt a slower economy and higher interest rates, together with less consumption; neither was a positive outlook.

Either solution to the deficit, then, would be a negative. What's more, the "progress" toward solving the deficit—which had been moved from $14 billion a month earlier in the year to $9 billion that

previous July, was no progress at all, Gross believed. "I think the problem is that we've reached
the point where no further progress is in store,"
he said. If the world lost confidence in the United
States' ability to progress on the trade deficit, he
said, the dollar might decline rapidly, forcing up
interest rates—and that could lead to a recession
and a stock market decline of another 200 to 400
points.

Gross added that he had recently had had dinner
with fed chief Volcker, who had told the Pimco
managing director he thought there was a "50-
50" chance the dollar might decline precipitously,
leading to higher interest rates and the accompany-
ing fallout. Gross had agreed: American investors
were not being realistic, he told the Los Angeles
paper. "There's no doubt in my mind," he said,
"that the crash was a warning shot across our bow,
our economic bow, so to speak, that our financial
books are not in order." To fix things, he said, the
deficit had to be addressed, and spending slowed
down; the personal savings rate (then 4 percent)
also needed to be bumped up—via (Gross's sugges-
tion) a tax on consumer items—to a savings rate of
(Gross's figure) 10 percent.

Since the crash, Gross added to the *L.A. Times*,
stock and bond prices had "moved in tandem,"
because bonds had become a competitive

investment with stocks and, at that moment in time, were yielding close to 9 percent. Investors had to sense that they could get at least 9 percent from a riskier plunge into stocks. But with dividend yields averaging 3 percent, investors would have to look for 6 percent annual appreciation or more—and that, Gross said, was the reason why stocks and bonds were linked.

By the time he gave another *New York Times* interview, the following month, November 1988, however, Gross was apparently feeling feisty again. "Bondholders have been taken advantage of for decades," he told the paper. "It's time they stood up and fought issuers and investment bankers who have taken advantage of them." At issue was the lawsuit John J. Creedon, chairman of the Metropolitan Life Insurance Company, had filed against F. Ross Johnson, CEO of the company then known as RJR Nabisco Inc. Creedon said his suit was intended to send a message to Johnson and other corporate execs and investment banks who, in his words, "rape[d]" bondholders as part of that era's takeover binge.

Johnson and Shearson Lehman Hutton Inc. of course had famously proposed a leveraged buyout of RJR, prompting its stock to skyrocket to $89, from $55. That was horrific news for bond markets for consumer companies; their individual and corporate bondholders now suffered big losses on paper, as investors began to fear that no company was safe from a similar takeover bid. Stockholders were being bought out—with a premium—and bonds were being turned into junk.

Shearson took particular heat. The firm had been one of the main underwriters for RJR's $300 million in bonds that spring. In October, however, Shearson itself became a principal investor in the proposed buyout, which immediately devalued those bonds. Bondholders in the buyouts using the most debt were losing an average 4 percent of their holdings. No wonder Gross & Co. were alarmed.

By the end of the decade, other concerns had arisen: worries about a recession, and the impact of the government's investigation of Drexel Burnham Lambert and the increasing yields on (below investment-grade-debt) "junk bonds," with the then-upcoming offering of securities by RJR Holdings to finance the largest leveraged buyout in history. Part of the government's look at Drexel entailed investigating the former head of its junk bond department, Michael Milken. And we all know how that ended: Milken, another "bond king," but one of greed, was indicted for securities fraud and racketeering in 1989 and sentenced to ten years in prison and a $600 million fine. This was the same guy who, that same decade, had approached Pimco, pitching his junk bonds. Chris Dialynas, Gross's right-hand man, was in charge of assessing that pitch. His recommendation: Pass. Pimco did just that.

Meanwhile, bond yields, which had fallen in the spring of 1986 to below 7.50 percent, their lowest point since the mid-1970s, started climbing again, to just under 10.25 percent. Then the October 1987 crash happened. By 1989 bond yields were down; interest rates were low; and corporate bonds, which had taken a blow from the RJR take-over, were once again stirring investor interest

For the first 10 months of 1989, according to a *New York Ti*mes report in November, corporate bonds rose by 15.6 percent on a total return basis, while Treasury issues, with a total return of 15.8 percent, did even better. Mortgage-backed securities rose by 15 percent, while high-yield "junk" issues posted a total return of about 4 percent.

Bill Gross must have been one happy fellow. His firm had upwards of $25 billion in assets to manage; business was brisk; and any reporter writing about bonds always made it a point to call the head of Pimco.

Chapter 3

The 1990s

(Even More) Fame and Fortune: Part 2

Media coverage in 1991 makes it clear that powerhouse Pimco had evolved by that point, early in the firm's third decade. Pimco's portfolios that year outperformed the Shearson Lehman government–corporate bond index by, on average, close to 250 basis points, according to *Institutional Investor*, looking back from 1992. In the ten years ended in 1991, Pimco was the top-performing bond manager among those taking comparable risk.

Certainly the firm had fuel in its tank; $32 billion in assets to manage for its parent company, Pacific Mutual. And clearly it had a well-deserved reputation for outstripping the competition: "Its track record is hard to beat," the *Orange County Register* observed that July. "In the fiscal year ended June 30, three of Pacific Mutual's bond funds ranked first, third and fifth in their respective groupings as ranked by Lipper Analytical Services."

But aside from pension funds managers and Wall Street, many individual investors remained in the dark about the firm, whose bond-management subsidiary, Pimco, had yet to reach its pinnacle of fame. "I have a lot of respect for them," Ian MacKinnon, chief bond manager for the Vanguard mutual funds, told the paper. "But a lot of folks just don't know who these guys are."

One reason for the knowledge gap was that Pacific Mutual's bond managers weren't reaching out to the little guy. There were no ad campaigns, no marketing, no PR staff or networks of commission-page brokers aimed at small investors, and the reason was clear: With big pension funds lining up at its door, the parent company couldn't be bothered with what the *Register* called "the large costs and headaches of bookkeeping for numerous small accounts." What PacMutual did want to spend energy on were the 16 mutual funds it had gathered by that point under an array of umbrella units favoring "P"-flavored acronyms:

- Pimco, which, the paper said, "handles the bulk of the money-management business"

- Pimit (Pacific Investment Management Investment Trust), which were mutual funds run by Pimco.

- Pfamco (Pacific Financial Asset Management Corp.): The units Pimco and Pimit carried the name Pfamco, which also had stock and real estate investment businesses.

"Pimco produces attractive returns by keeping its costs low, eschewing bets on interest rates and talking long-term views of economic situations," the *Register* wrote. Though PacMutual had only started its mutual fund business in 1987 "as a natural extension of Pimco's institutional money management business," it was already the eighth largest pension fund manager.

Its principals apparently felt little need to reach out to small investors. Most of them couldn't afford it, in any case. The minimum investment for a Pimit fund was $500,000; $200,000 for Pfamco. Alternately, an investor who fancied buying equities might, for a mere $200,000, jump into one or more of eight newly minted (as of spring 1991) stock funds run by independent stock-picking subsidiaries or two income funds run by PacMutual's bond managers.

As Charles Schwab or Harbor Bond Fund customers, investors *could* get in on PacMutual's action—indirectly at least—with $1,000 or $2,000 respective minimum investments. But that was about it for the "little" guys.

Pimit Total Return—which was the most popular pick at the time, had $1.1 billion in assets, and returned 12.67 percent—"employed," the *Register* wrote, "the same basic strategy that Pacific Mutual's pension clients get to maximize returns—using a wide spectrum of income-producing notes from U.S. Treasury issues to lower-rated (but not junk) bonds to foreign securities."

Junk bonds, of course, would have been undignified for a firm that was obviously going places.

★★★★★

Pimit Total Return may have been the most popular, but the Total Return Fund was coming up fast. "Gross pays little attention to categories, investing wherever he sees a good deal," *Forbes* magazine wrote in 1993. As of February of that year, the Total Return Fund Gross managed had an ecletic mix among its top five holdings: 30-year Treasury bond futures, eight-year French government bonds, collateralized mortgage obligations from the Resolution Trust Co., 30-year senior bonds of AMR Corp., and 11 1/8 percent debentures issued by CTC Mansfield, an Ohio coal company. This was not to overlook smaller paper holdings from the Canadian Wheat Board and the Province of Alberta. About 40 percent of these assets were in bond futures, one third from abroad, as Gross surmised that interest rates would keep dropping.

Though still a subsidiary of PacMutual, Pimco
had its eye on growth: In August 1993 it announced it was launching a real estate investment
trust (REIT), with hopes of raising $150 million
in an IPO of its new Pimco Commercial Mortgage
Securities Trust Inc. That entity was set up to
own securities backed by the mortgages of office
buildings, shopping centers, warehouses, hotels,
and hospitals. The move was unusual: REITs, a
hot investment trend at the time, usually invest in
securities backed by home mortgages.

In March, 1994, the *Wall Street Journal* reported
Pimco's merger with the much smaller Thomson
Advisory Group LP; this strategy created "one of
the largest publicly traded money-management
firms in the U.S., with about $70 billion in assets,"
noted the *WSJ*.

Pimco probably found good use for those assets
a mere month later, in April, when sudden good
news in the nation's nonfarm payroll numbers—in
the wake of two federal increases in short-term interest rates—set off a wave of bond sales; the price
of the 30-year bond had sunk 11 3/8 points; yield
was up to 7.26 percent. The *Wall Street Journal*
quoted Gross as saying that Pimco still had about
$10 billion, or 20 percent of its total holdings, in
30-year Treasuries, but to protect itself against
further interest rate increases, it had recently sold

off $750 million in mortgage-backed securities and put 30 percent of its total holdings into cash. "Everything helps when you're trying to keep your head above water," Gross told the paper.

He said—or postured—that he wasn't worried. With lots of cash on hand, his firm could weather the bear market, he said, predicting that it would stay that way up to a year and that long-term interest rates would peak at 7.5 percent before a turnaround.

Another indicator of change was Pimco's hiring, in April, 1993, of William S. Thompson as co-chief executive and managing director. Following a transition, Thompson stepped in for Bill Podlich, who, of course, had been one of Gross's original cofounders. Podlich, Pimco said, would now work on "long-range planning and outside activities" while Thompson would oversee day-to-day operations. (An executive told *Barron's* that Podlich's move did not indicate dissatisfaction with his performance.)

Interestingly, Thompson had been the chair of the Asia division of Salomon Brothers, a firm that Pimco probably felt little love for, following an infamous, if derailed, "joke" in 1991. That year, the former head of Salomon's government bond unit arranged to have a Pimco employee submit a fake bid of $1 billion to a Salomon sales person who was retiring. A little retirement send-off, as it were.

The timing for the prank was bizarre, considering that Salomon the previous month had admitted violating federal rules at five Treasury auctions, and top execs had resigned. Pimco was just as unforgiving; it suspended business with the Wall Street giant; and subsequently, Salomon—well, everyone knows what happened to Salomon.

So Thompson got out in good time. And after taking the reins at Pimco as operations CEO, he had plenty to do. First on the agenda: The firm began to wean itself from its parent, Pacific Mutual. In 1994, Pimco shares began to trade publicly and gain more access for sales to small investors. It had gone public after helping to create the new limited partnership Pimco Advisors LLP.

The Thomson merger, meanwhile, called for Pacific Mutual and its subsidiary Pimco to pay $140 million to certain shareholders of Thomson, a Connecticut-based mutual fund company, letting those shareholders and key insiders own 17 percent of the new concern. The limited partnership would then control the money-management businesses at both PacMutual (five money-management companies, including Pimco) and Thomson (three). The Pimco executive who played a key role in the merger was its former vice chairman and CIO, Bill Cvengros.

The move, which Pimco on its website described as a reverse merger of its holding company, made the new Pimco Advisors a bigger mutual fund concern than such existing entities as Dreyfus and Putnam. As for financing, Pimco on its own brought $54 billion into the merger.

And now its managers were about to take a chunk of that home. "As a private company, we had limitations on how far we could go in financial incentives for key management personnel," Cvengros told the *Orange County Register*. "Being a public company gives us another tool for providing incentives for management retention." He added that his intention was to let Pimco's money managers do what they did best: manage money, and personal profit.

"The rich are about to get a whole lot richer," the *Register* crowed that October, 1994 after an SEC filing divulged that Gross and nine colleagues in Newport Beach were about to divvy up $120 million in stock from the merger. One less happy result of that move: Pimco Advisors would now have to pay corporate income taxes, and shareholders would have to pay personal income tax on dividend income.

Still another result of the merger: Those individual investors who previously couldn't afford to invest in Gross's vision now could do just that.

Things just kept getting better for Pimco, even if the global picture wasn't always encouraging (think: the ruble crisis, the Asian crisis, the devaluation of the Mexican peso). In 1996 the firm expanded into Asia by opening a Singapore office. In 1997 it gained a foothold in Europe, opening a London office. Subsequent new offices were established in Tokyo and Sydney.

By the late 1990s, according to Pimco's website, the firm had $100 billion in assets and 500 employees. The firm was also trying new things: In 1997 it was one of the first to deal in Treasury inflation-protected securities, or TIPS. According to its website, Pimco also upped its array of asset strategies with its dive into emerging markets bonds and municipal bonds.

Earlier, in 1992, a feature story in *Institutional Investor* (flatteringly headlined "The Pimco Magic") had detailed the smart moves that lay behind Pimco's rapid expansion. Journalist Julie Rohrer wrote how, guided by such intellectual lights as economists Robert Reich and Paul Krugman, Pimco took on a "bullish assessment" in 1991 that "proved right on target." Anticipating slow growth in the economy and the rate of inflation, as well as the Fed's moves to stimulate the economy—and bring interest rates down in the process, creating a higher yield—Rohrer wrote, "Pimco decided to go for broke."

In 1990 the firm lengthened durations for its portfolios to five-and-a-half years, a real stretch for Pimco, considering its history up to that point. The firm then spent oodles of cash, placing close to 10 percent of its accounts in such unusual places as money-center bank bonds selling at discount.

The strategy was a stunning success, as Pimco outperformed the Shearson Lehman government/corporate bond index, on average, by close to 250 basis points.

In pension management, including equities as well as fixed income, "Pimco stands alone," Rohrer wrote. "Most of its returns come from forecasting the economy and the course of interest rates. . . And all along it has not only adapted to changes in the bond markets but also proved a leader in introducing them."

Not that any of this happened overnight, Rohrer pointed out. Only when the market bottomed out in the 1980s and rates peaked did the explosion of explosive growth in fixed-income securities occur, fueling the wave that Gross et al. were now riding in the '90s. "Today more than $4 trillion is invested," Rohrer wrote in 1992, "not just in corporate and governments but in a dizzying array of mortgage-backed securities, collateralized mortgage obligations, strips, interest-only and principal-only securities and various bond hybrids, not to mentioned fixed-income derivatives. The quantitative wizards of Wall Street have created a steady stream of specialized products, quantitative tools, and portfolio-structuring techniques that offer institutions just about any approach to the fixed-income market that suits their strategic fancy." Bonds were surging, she wrote, and Pimco stood at the head of the class pack in managing them.

BusinessWeek also published an adoring piece about Pimco's Gross. "The Peter Lynch of Bonds?" it asked (seemingly rhetorically, but it was actually echoing mutual fund analysts) in May, 1994, intoning the name of the mutual fund world's greatest investor (Lynch famously produced 29 percent returns for his portfolios for 13 years straight).

Pimco by that point, reported *BW* writer Jeffrey Laderman, had $55 billion in assets to play with and since 1974 had earned an annual average return of 11.1 percent—versus 9.6 percent for the Lehman Brothers Government/Corporate Bond Index. Bonds had been severely down across the board that year of 1994—the worst for bonds in six decades, some sources said—and Pimco was no exception; but *its* "down," 2.8 percent, still beat the index's 3.1 percent.

Money magazine joined the fan club that July, headlining its profile of Gross (alongside Dan Fuss of Loomis Sayles, the Boston-based mutual fund), "Two Titans Clash on the Best Way to Make Money in Bonds." Gross, the magazine said, saw 30-year Treasurys hovering in the range of 6 percent to 8 percent for the new few years. So, investors should stop worrying about the direction of rates and instead go for yields by choosing bonds with maturities longer than 10 years, and employ selective buying of lower-quality bonds and foreign issues, the magazine said. This contrasted, *Money* said, with the proclivities of Fuss, who was still intent on capital gains and as such sought bonds and convertible securities with depressed prices; these companies would recover with economic growth, bringing rising returns, Fuss believed.

Bonds' tough times in 1994 led to a rally in May, 1995 followed by a sell-off in March, 1996. "Temporary Insanity in Bonds," *BusinessWeek* headlined one article, reporting that, in the space of two weeks, prices had plunged nearly $50 on each $1,000 bond, driving yield on the benchmark 30-year Treasury from 6.03 percent to 6.47 percent. "We had thought the next general move in interest rates would be up,"

Ian MacKinnon of Vanguard Group told the magazine, "but we were not prepared for the magnitude or the suddenness of the move."

Gross, the long-term investor he was, had a more optimistic, less bearish, view. "We're still on the long-term secular path of disinflation," he said. "Nothing's changed in recent weeks that would alter that." In short, it was time for a correction and the realization that the tendency in those days for hedge funds to buy U.S. Treasurys in bulk had to soften a bit. Other factors at that point in the 1990s included an apparent drop in confidence that Senator Bob Dole would be the Republican presidential candidate (Dole espoused strong support for a balanced budget, which would be good for bonds) and that the Fed would ease rates much more. (Dole of course was the 1996 GOP candidate but didn't win.)

By May, the rollercoaster had eased and bonds were being touted (by *BusinessWeek* at least) as "a good hedge against the overheated stock market as well as a nice spot to stash cash."

Indeed, although bond funds earned only 4.5 cents of each of the $168.4 billion outlays that long-term, open-end mutual funds attracted during the first eight months of the year, *Barron's* in October reported some good news: A number of "hot emerging-market funds" had been "besting most equity mutual funds," the magazine said. The Investment Company Institute was even saying that high-yield bond funds had received cash inflows of $6.95 billion through August, accounting for most of the total $7.64 billion bond funds had attracted in the first eight months of that year. Of the four bond funds that had received such net flows, no surprise, one from Pimco—its Total Ret A—was number one.

By late 1997, things had calmed down quite a bit. A *Forbes* article that month called Pimco's consensus "optimistic for bonds," though the publication also called the firm's foray into equity portfolios one of "limited success"—with only $22 billion under management in that division. "The company plans to expand that effort," *Forbes* revealed, describing a pending $262 million acquisition of a controlling stake in the $60 billion Oppenheimer Capital investment management commune.

In a December Q&A with *Money* magazine, Gross was still calm and collected, despite bond investors' nervousness that then-Fed Chairman Alan Greenspan was hinting at an interest rate hike to stave off inflation. *Money* described Pimco Total Return's assets as standing at $532 million and producing an average annual gain of 10.48 percent. You're still bullish about bonds (despite Greenspan's warning)? *Money* asked the Bond King. Gross replied that 30-year Treasurys had been yielding about 6.5 percent, representing—considering the 2 percent inflation rate—a real interest rate of 4.5 percent and "a fairly wide spread."

"Our expectations are that inflation will remain under control for the balance of the century— which is key because inflation is the enemy of the bond investor," Gross continued. He cited global forces, like increased competition among countries and technological breakthroughs that he thought would keep prices down. The federal budget was also moving toward a balance, meaning there was little reason to expect the government to issue any new debt on a net basis, he said.

And while he acknowledged that threats of inflation were still lurking, he described an "era of 6 percent," meaning that the super bull markets of the past in stocks and bonds couldn't continue. Bond investors would receive the interest from their investments and a little bit of price appreciation, meaning, for Treasury notes, a return of about 6 percent, he predicted, adding that he expected something similar in stocks.

In 1997, Gross's new book, *Everything You've Heard About Investing Is Wrong!* reiterated this prediction of muted returns, the end of the "Era of Money," and of the bull market. He defended this stance in a year-end/decade's-end interview, again, with *Money* magazine, in December, 1999. "In this type of global environment, in which disinflation—and in some cases deflation—dominates, it's almost impossible to manufacture 20 percent to 30 percent returns from the stock market," Gross told his interviewer. "That doesn't suggest you should stuff your money in the mattress. It simply means you should lower your expectations. After all, in a world of 1 percent inflation, you're doing pretty well if you're getting returns of 6 percent to 8 percent from stocks and bonds." He said he calculated the number 6 percent by figuring that that had been the typical growth rate of corporate profits over the previous 50 years; he then added on another 1 percent to 2 percent in dividend growth for stocks.

For bonds, he said, "We've achieved much of the decline in yields that I've been looking for. It's not that we can't go lower, but I think we are close to the bottom of a 17-year bull market in bonds. I don't think yields are headed back up."

In the interview Gross referred to his heroes, J.P. Morgan, Bernard Baruch, and 1920s trader Jesse Livermore. Under a picture of Livermore he had on his office wall, Gross said, was this quote: "In actual practice, an investor has to guard against many things. And most of all, against himself."

An echo of this warning seemed apparent in an article titled, "How Gross Games the Indexes," which appeared in *Institutional Investor* in 1998. Although Gross was named "Morningstar Fixed Income Manager of the Year" that year (an honor repeated in 2000 and 2007), there were some stirrings of concern. *Institutional Investor*'s Alyssa Lappen was among those voicing them. "Critics argue that size alone has forced Pimco to branch into risky new sectors," she wrote. "Gross has been incredibly savvy about metamorphosing his portfolios and style," she said a former employee had told her. "In the early '80s Pimco made interest rate bets, pure and simple. When the portfolios got to about $10 billion, Gross began taking sector bets. In the late '90s he added futures arbitrage, and then he moved into high yield and international. Pimco couldn't manage $148 billion and substantially add value just in corporate bonds."

Pimco's clients tolerated these new ventures in a way equities clients might not, the article pointed out. But not everything was totally rosy. The firm had lost seasoned managers, including a 14-year veteran who'd created its issue-selection analysis and its "Stocks Plus" manager. His loss cut the firm's number of experienced bond generalists from five to three during a period of big growth.

So the question begged: was there a ceiling to growth? "Sheer size and style shifts could eventually hurt," Lappen pointed out, "since, as the boilerplate goes, past performance doesn't guarantee future success."

Chapter 4

The Early 2000s

From 9/11 Tragedy to Subprime Shenanigans

Just prior to the start of the new millennium, in November, 1999, the *Wall Street Journal* announced what The Street had been expecting for months: Allianz AG, the big German insurer, had bought a 70 percent stake in Pimco Advisors Holdings LP, paying $38.75 a share. That represented a 12 percent premium over the firm's then-share price of $34.6875—which itself had skyrocketed after news of the talks between the new partners broke the previous summer.

Everyone was a winner in this deal. Pimco Advisors, the operating company overseeing seven subsidiaries and $260 billion in assets, would now join with Allianz's $360 billion, to create one of the world's biggest money managers.

Following the purchase, the entity of Pimco Advisors LP would disappear into a new holding company (no longer public but retaining the Pimco name) split between California and Munich. German executive Joachim Faber would become CEO of Allianz Asset Management and William Thompson would be president of Pacific Management. Pimco alone brought $180 billion in assets to the deal, including Total Return Fund's $30 billion.

Not everyone made the transition, however: Former CEO William Cvengros left Pimco to head a software developer because, the *Orange County Business Journal* reported, with Pimco losing its public status, Cvengros's forte, investor relations, was no longer needed. (Gross insisted that the firm urged the CEO to stay.)

Pimco's longtime owner, Pacific Mutual Life Insurance, since renamed Pacific Life, would stay in the game, retaining a 30 percent ownership. Allianz also got what it wanted: the kind of U.S. presence its rivals (e.g., AXA, Zurich Financial Services Group), already enjoyed. Last but hardly least was the acquisition of Pimco's star manager, Bill Gross. "Everyone's keen to acquire the skills of a U.S. fund manager," Michael Lindsay of Lehman Brothers in London told the *Journal*. After all, among U.S. fund managers, Gross *was* the Bond King, considering how Pimco produced a reliable, steady income. In 1999's third quarter, the

WSJ reported, the firm reported record net new customer inflows of $6.9 billion and strong profits. According to Morningstar Inc. research, the Total Return Fund had ranked in the top 3 percent in its category over the previous three, five and 10 years, with an annual return (over 10 years) of 9 percent.

Gross himself certainly benefited handsomely from the Allianz deal. According to a proxy, he was set to be paid $39.8 million in stock and cash annually, plus $5 million a year in restricted stock for five years on top of his regular, undisclosed salary. Certainly Allianz would have accepted the fact that it had to pay big-time to lock in Gross's services. According to the *WSJ*, the managing director and his staff at that time managed $180 billion in bond assets, including more than $40 billion in mutual funds, representing an eye-popping 5 percent of those assets industrywide.

Those numbers had grown considerably since 1990, when Pimco managed just $25 billion. Gross's Total Return Fund alone had produced an average 9.18 percent total return for the previous 10 years, topping by 108 basis points the Lehman Brothers Aggregate Bond index for that period.

Meanwhile, there was another plus to this deal for the Europeans: "A move like this gets people on board who will bring something to the table from day one," Lehman's Lindsay told the *Journal*. Getting people on board was important, he explained, because Europe's state social security systems were crumbling and European workers anticipating retirement were turning to the private sector.

Yet another benefit Pimco itself received, on top of the obvious financial ones, was the ability to retain its master-limited partnership structure, enabling it to avoid paying 35 percent corporate income tax on profits, and instead pay a rather more modest 3.5 percent tax on revenue.

Pimco further gained the ability to move more quickly into the international fund markets. The firm already had outposts in Japan, Singapore, Australia and parts of Europe at this point. During the 2000s, the firm would open offices in Hong Kong and Toronto (followed by Milan in 2012), expand into real estate investment trusts (REITs), and grow its assets to $1 trillion, managed by a staff which had grown to 1,000 employees.

★★★★★

Of course, for anyone of majority age, the most important, and gut-wrenching, event of those years was (and remains) the 9/11 Attack on America. Gross, the investment guy, was hardly insensitive to those emotions. In an "Investment Outlook" written the following Sunday, just before

the reopening of NYSE, he quoted from Leonard
Cohen's dirge *Anthem* and actually worked in a
financial angle. When he was a boy, Gross wrote,
his parents still had war bonds, savings bonds,
Treasury bonds. "Now, " he lamented, "instead of
savings bonds, we equate patriotism with support-
ing the price of CISCO at $14 a share and making
sure the malls are full of shoppers pushing each
other aside in order to purchase the newest upgrade
of Nintendo.

"Strange, isn't it—how we've changed, what we
consider to be important, how dependent we've
become on consumerism and the 'market,'" Gross
continued. He regretted that transformation, he
said, "although I've done more than my fair share
to support it."He went on to pose the question,
"buy or save?" and to worry whether and when the
nation would be willing to take chances again and
to take risk "which is and has been the essence of
our capitalistic society for centuries." Bond King
that he was, he pointed out that the bond market
had reopened days before, to a "stunning, but not
unexpected rally."

★★★★★

The Allianz deal had been scheduled to close in
March, 2000 but the shareholder vote was delayed
until April due to inaction by the SEC (the State of
California also initially threatened a delay because

Allianz allegedly wasn't making required payments to Holocaust survivors).

There was further concern about the then-volatility on Wall Street. Even Pimco, which seemed unassailable, couldn't escape investor jitters. During the fourth quarter of 1999 customers took more money out of Pimco's funds than they put in, the *Orange County Register* reported. That was the first quarterly net outflow in the firm's history and raised concerns that Pimco might not make its revenue target to enable the Allianz deal to proceed (concerns that Pimco pooh-poohed).

But these were mere road bumps. Other good things were happening for Pimco. Its managing director, who had become a media darling, supervised the construction of an in-house TV studio, "the latest corporate status symbol," *Fortune* opined, adding, "Today, when Gross is called to pontificate on the market, he saunters down the hall."

No surprise, the Allianz deal brought internal changes. Some Pimco employees were sent to Munich to open a fixed-income office for Europe, and Allianz employees were transferred to Newport Beach. With Allianz's transfer of $100 billion in assets to Pimco, the firm's assets soared to $300 billion under management, the *Orange County Register* reported. The firm would also retain its managing board of directors, who signed long-term contracts. "We wanted to make sure that Allianz couldn't reach in and change the successful formula that we've been able to use for the past 25 years," Gross said. "We're certainly not adopting the Allianz style of money management."

Clearly, he looked forward to an era of growth. "If we hadn't had Allianz, we would have moved much more slowly, globally," Gross said. "Our presence on the continent would probably have been five years from now instead of five months."

Added Bill Thompson, in the same interview, "We certainly could see the day when we top a trillion dollars, but that's down the road a few years."

★★★★★

So what does a man do with all those millions? Early in the 2000s, publications were reporting that Bill Gross was worth $443 million—a sum composed of $40 million a year for five years (per the Allianz deal), plus a $243 million windfall for selling his stake in Pimco.

But beyond his really nice car and really nice oceanfront home, Gross and his family (he's been married to his second wife, Sue Frank, since 1985; they have a son, and Gross has a son and daughter from his first marriage) liked to keep a low profile. "Mr. Gross generally prefers beer and meatloaf and insists the family stay at $50-a-night Holiday Inns when they take their 11-year-old son Nick to Quebec to play in hockey tournaments," the *National Post* wrote.

"The mild-mannered Catholic convert is the first to admit that $443 million is too much money for anyone."

Instead of an over-the-top lifestyle, Gross chose a quiet life with a focus on physical fitness. He quit running marathons at age fifty but was very much into yoga, prompting *Newsweek* in 2001 to interview the then-57-year-old bond king for a feature on men's entry into yoga's mostly female universe. "To me, yoga is great physical training, not something spiritual or religious," Gross told the magazine. "I want to be as effective as I can in my job. It's results-driven. And the results have been remarkable."

Besides family, two other things absorbed Gross's personal time. One was (and is) philanthropy, with an emphasis on education and health care. In January, 2005 he and Sue donated $20 million to a new women's pavilion at Hoag Memorial Hospital in Newport Beach. They had already been major donors for 11 years, giving $100,000 for the Orange County Teacher of the Year program and establishing a $3 million foundation at Sage Hill School in Newport Coast for scholarships for disadvantaged

students. But 2005 was the year the couple formalized their charitable commitments, founding the
William and Sue Gross Family Foundation.

"We're sort of turning our attention from making
money to donating it in a proper way to benefit the
community," Gross told the *Register.*

The Grosses would go on to solidify their mark in
philanthropy, donating $23.5 million to Bill's alma
mater, Duke University, whose scholarship aid had
enabled him to attend as a young man.

Then there was Bill Gross's *other* interest, which
had nothing to do with either philanthropy or
bonds: stamps. Yes, stamps. In November, 2005
he became only the third collector ever to form a
complete collection of 19th century U.S. stamps.
He purchased at auction that October, a unique
plate block for a 1918 24-cent U.S. airmail run—
featuring an (accidentally) upside-down printing of
a biplane. Gross paid $2.97 million for the block,
then traded it to a dealer for a 1-cent 1868 "Z
Grill" Benjamin Franklin stamp—to complete his
19th century collection.

This was big news in the philatelic world.

So was the announcement, in 2007, that
Gross, having become the first collector to own
one of every U.S. stamp issued, was auction-

ing off his collection of British stamps, valued at as much as $5 million, to benefit Doctors Without Borders.

★★★★★

Meanwhile, back in the financial world, investor nervousness over stocks toward the end of 2001, caused a mega-switch to bond funds, which of course was good for the Pimco Total Return Fund. It passed the $50 billion mark, almost overtaking the leader, Investment Company of America, a stock fund with $51.37 billion in assets, the *Milwaukee Journthal Sentinel* reported.

The S&P 500 index had been down through that November, but the Lehman Brothers' long Treasury bond index was up, and corporate bonds rose 11.4 percent.

What's bad for stocks is good for bonds. Pimco Total Return, which had not posted a calendar year loss since 1977—despite a bad stretch the first half of the year when it trailed competitors—reported a 10.6 percent gain. That gain beat 84 percent of other bond funds in the same category, including Pimco's two larger competitors, the Vanguard 500 Index Fund and Fidelity Magellan Fund.

Pimco's success was attributed by financial experts to its emphasis on total return rather than yield. Indeed, in his post-9/11 commentary, Gross said that, "Victory generally belongs to the risk takers, but a risk taker must pick his spots and his price. Prices are not right at the moment for taking big chances either in bonds or in stocks."

★★★★★

In August, 2002, the Pimco Total Return Fund became the largest actively managed mutual fund, besting Fidelity's Magellan Fund, long the big banana of the fund groups. Total Return had $61.2 billion in assets under management on July 31, $1.3 billion more than the $59.9 billion Magellan Fund—if anyone was counting (they were). "Who'd have thunk it?" CEO Bill Thompson told Knight Ridder Tribune Business News.

Magellan had fallen, at that point in 2002, by 23.2 percent, a drop blamed on Wall Street's three years-in-a-row decline, causing investors to switch to more stable equity funds or abandon stocks and move to money market or bond funds. Total Return, in contrast, fell only by 5 percent because its strategy was based on performance rather than fund flows.

"There's no question that some investors who are alarmed by the stock market have found their way into our funds," Thompson told the news service. "But our growth has been steady. It hasn't really spiked. There's a recognition that diversification makes an enormous amount of sense. I think that's here to stay."

Yet Pimco couldn't claim the largest mutual fund. That honor belonged to the Vanguard 500 Index Fund, a passively managed fund that duplicates the S&P 500; its assets as of July 31, 2002 were $86.3 billion.

Still, despite its new mantle of success, Pimco and its managers knew there wasn't all that much reason to celebrate, because bonds—like everything else in a gloomy and, at this point, war-torn financial world, where the Fed had cut the interest rate to 1.75 percent—were rocky. Bonds lose value as interest rates rise and these rates had nowhere to go but up (if they ever would); plus, there were all those possible corporate defaults out there that could lose investors principal. Indeed, in reports that fall of 2002, Pimco made good on its decision to cut corporate bond holdings; its funds held about 17 percent of corporate bonds—in contrast to 35 percent in a typical bond fund.

In interviews at the time, Pimco managers also said they were steering clear of high-yield junk bonds—too risky. They viewed municipal bonds as risky because some municipalities were having a hard time making debt payments—though even those difficulties paled beside the risk corporate bondholders faced.

And mortgage bonds? They might seem safe—
backed as they are by quasi-government guarantees
and (at that time) rates above Treasurys'. Yet their
performance could be hurt by both rising and falling interest rates.

Overall, bonds' 20-year rally was over. "We've lost
the wind that's been at our backs for the last couple
of decades," Dan Fuss of Loomis Sayles Bond
Fund told the publication, *Financial Planning*,
referring to various factors—war, a hike in taxes to
pay for it, and the economic boom in China—that
augured a rise in inflation accompanied by a rise in
interest rates.

In a hint of what was to come a few years down
the road, Pimco Fed watcher Paul McCulley told
the *Orange County Register* that while the firm still
owned a lot of mortgages, "You have to say that
mortgages are getting close to the end of their
party." If rates rose and homeowners stopped
refinancing, "then mortgages are not going to be
pleasant over the next couple of years [as mortgage
bonds would fall in value]."

★★★★★

At the same time that he shied away from financial
risk, Bill Gross was not a man to shy away from
political risk. Around this time, early in the 2000s,
he made waves by claiming that the Dow, which he

considered overvalued, would need to fall to 5,000 to represent fair value. The equity community was not happy about that. Wrote Gross in his usual take-no-prisoners style: "Stocks stink and will continue to do so until they are priced appropriately, probably somewhere around Dow 5000, S&P 650, or Nasdaq God knows where."

Gross took a risk again by criticizing the ethics at General Electric, one of Pimco's clients, actually, for not being clear on its decision to tap the bond market. He wrote in a commentary that he believed former CEO Jack Welch, and then-current CEO Jeffrey Immelt, had not been "totally forthcoming" about how they were able to increase earnings at close to 15 percent per year for the previous several decades. GE had too little of its short-term debt backed up by bank lines of credit, Gross said. Also, it was too reliant on its "money machine," GE Capital, even as it boosted earnings by acquiring other companies, using GE stock and commercial paper, creating a structure with "near hedge fund" leverage levels. The industrial giant should be more forthcoming with investors, Gross wrote, practically baiting GE (which did not withdraw its money from Pimco although its stock did take a dive).

Gross further criticized the war in Iraq, prompting criticism that he was trying to steer investors toward his portfolio makeup: He'd been shifting away from Treasurys, which do well in wartime, into corporate bonds, which could suffer.

Finally, Pimco's managing director suggested around this time that directors' remuneration at companies should be tied to the level of bond spread over Treasurys. This would mirror the rewards given for increasing the price of stock.

By August, 2003, when the long-term bull market had given way to the beginnings of a bear market— never good for bonds—Gross sat for an interview with the *New York Times*, in which he rejected a reporter's observation that he had gone from being on top to being on the bottom. Gross described a different perspective. "Let me put it this way," he said. "The best investment performance is when you're outperforming the market and the market is doing well. That's when you deliver not only relative money to your clients but absolute money. You feel super-duper; you feel good. Now we're doing better than the market, which is good, but clients are beginning to lose money. That doesn't feel as good."

Further elaborating on his philosophy, Gross said, "The worst is where your clients are losing absolute money and relative money. In other words, you're underperforming the market. That would send me into absolute depression."

★★★★★

The latter 2000s were a time when the financial press began to take notice of Mohamed El-Erian. The Cambridge- and Oxford-educated, Egyptian-born El-Erian (who'd settled in the United States in 1983), was in his early 40s when he joined Pimco in 1999. There he became a senior member of the firm's portfolio management and investment strategy group. (He left in 2006 to manage Harvard University's endowment, but quickly returned, just a year later.)

From his perch at Pimco, El-Erian frequently contributed thought pieces on finance to leading publications. He also wrote a best-selling book, *When Markets Collide: Investment Strategies for the Age of Global Economic Change* (McGraw-Hill, 2008). With his international background, his doctorate in economics, and a background doing emerging-markets work for the International Monetary Fund, he was the perfect man to oversee that part of the business at Pimco. Indeed, *Forbes* noted his "masterful performance" as head of the Emerging Markets Bond Fund, where he produced an 18.8 percent annual return over five years.

In an intriguing interview with *SmartMoney* in February, 2006, while at Harvard, El-Erian discussed some of the indicators that were even then pointing to the housing-finance crisis we know from hindsight was going to come. He was asked, for instance, about the then "almost flat" yield curve—meaning Treasury bonds weren't yielding much more than very-short-term issues—typically a sign, the reporter pointed out, of a coming recession. "Are you worried?"she asked El-Erian.

"In the old days, when you would have asked a domestic question, I would have given a domestic answer," he responded. Instead, the yield curve was now controlled less by the Fed than by the Asian central banks buying the lion's share of Treasurys, he said. In addition, most of the lending was no longer sensitive to the overnight rate because it was the result less of banking institutions than non-banking mortgage companies, which were bundling those mortgages and selling them as securities. "This means that you can no longer interpret the curve in the old way," El-Erian said.

At this point (2006), the Chinese, for example, were buying Treasurys, regardless of price, out of self-interest, El-Erian says. They wanted their "export machine" to grow and create jobs for their own people, and to capture market share as well as attract multinational factories.

Meanwhile, the Fed was raising interest rates, El-Erian continued, not to influence bonds, but to try to dampen the housing market where, in a state like California, more than 80 percent of the mortgages issued over the previous 12 months had been interest-only loans. "The only way people can afford to buy is through these exotic mortgages," El-Erian said, and the Fed was seeking some way to slow down that trend, which was being fueled by all the nonbanking sources selling them—sources the Fed couldn't control.

★★★★★

Regardless of El-Erian's statements, Pimco was investing heavily in mortgage-backed securities. A January, 2007 story in the *Los Angeles Times* noted that Pimco had allocated more than half of its $100 billion Total Return Fund to mortgage bonds and reduced its holdings of Treasurys to 7 percent. And why not? The higher interest rates on the mortgages gave the securities attractive rates of returns.

Meanwhile, the ABX index, which tracked the cost of insuring BBB-minus-rated bonds backed by mortgages to borrowers with poor credit histories—the so-called subprime market—indicated that the cost of insuring these bonds had sharply increased. A plunge of 30 percent by the end of February indicated that the market saw risky mortgage bonds as likely to lose their value, as defaults in the loans backing them rose.

"It reflects a disaster in the making in subprime, and I think it's just going to get worse," Nouriel Roubini, chairman of economics research website

"Roubini Global Economics," and a professor at
New York University, told the *WSJ*. Daniel Ivascyn, a Pimco portfolio manager, meanwhile, was
asked his view of the housing market and borrowers' ability to pay their mortgages. Answering carefully, he replied that selling insurance at that point
was "probably a good bet..." but, he added, in an
obvious reference to the ABX index, "...not neces-
sarily a slam dunk."

★★★★★

*Subprime Anguish: Recent market events have Wall
Street on notice,* warned a headline that March
in *Investment Dealers Digest*. Would the effects of
deteriorating subprime loans remain confined to
just a few firms, or spread? In a February report, a
Merrill Lynch analyst, Edward Najarian, predicted
that losses would rise throughout 2007 but have
a minor effect on large-cap regional banks, the
largest mortgage lenders. Subprime loans made up
12 to 14 percent of Wells Fargo's portfolio and 8.5
percent of National City's, Najarian estimated, but
constituted 3 percent or less of other large regional
institutions.

"The large Wall Street firms also appear to be
protected from consumer-loan fallout," the article
opined. Michael Hecht, an analyst with Bank of
America Securities, reported that Wall Street firms
such as Lehman Brothers and Bear Stearns were
in the "moving and shipping" business and held

relatively little in the way of mortgage-backed securities (MBS) and asset-backed securities (ABS) on their books.

Scott Simon, who headed MBS at Pimco, also chimed in. "A lot of lenders stopped making money a few years ago, so they had to make a decision: Do we keep making loans at lower credit quality, or stop making them altogether?" he asked. "If they stopped making them, they would go out of business. So they continued making loans and hoped they wouldn't go bad."

Those hopes were quickly dashed. Borrowers who never should have been approved were receiving enormous loans whose terms quickly escalated beyond what they'd been led to expect. Interest rates approached 12 percent—twice what a credit-worthy borrower would be charged. Not only that, but the aggressive lending practices of those years were also being applied to Alt-A mortgages, which fall between subprime and prime loans. UBS data showed that the default rate for that mid tier had doubled in 14 months, according to *Investment Dealers Digest*, with 2.4 percent of those loans 60 days past due, compared with the subprime sector's 10.5 percent delinquency rate.

Financial strategists began to worry that a flood of foreclosed homes could be put up for sale and push down prices. "The big question," Richard Gilhooly, a senior fixed income strategist at BNP Paribas, told FT.com, "is, how quickly will housing prices adjust lower as delinquency rates rise?" Lehman Brothers, of all sources, projected that mortgage defaults could reach $225 billion during 2007 and 2008 and perhaps go as high as $300 billion.

Delinquency rates for subprime adjustable-rate mortgages hit 14.4 per cent, and the numbers threatened to get worse as borrowers began to face a "reset" of their adjustable rate mortgages (ARMs) which they couldn't refinance. Indeed, Lehman estimated that more than $900 billion of mortgages would be reset in the next two years. Investors began waking up to the fact that they themselves owned subprime mortgages through complex collateralized debt obligation (CDO) packages of asset-backed bonds. Yet, because buyers relied on credit ratings to know when to sell, and those ratings lagged market prices, their losses were greater than they would have been once the credit rating downgrade occurred. As a result, investors began dumping shares of home loan lenders. Hovering in the background was the threat that credit requirements throughout all the markets would be tightened.

The word "recession" began to enter the conversation.

Bill Gross, not surprisingly, chose this point to
weigh in, in his March, 2007 "Investment Outlook," entitled "Grim Reality." After mourning
what he called the end of a "20% down reality that
[had] morphed somehow into a subprime/Alt A
cyberspace free-for-all," he wrote that the problem
with the U.S. housing market wasn't subprime
delinquencies or defaults. He even predicted that
"foreclosure losses as a percentage of existing loans
will be small," noting (in his view) homeowners
"substantial equity" in their homes.

"Analysts and pundits now claim we're out of the
woods," he wrote. "The subprime crisis is or has
been isolated and identified for what it is—a small
part of the U.S. economy." It would not be loan
losses threatening the U.S. economy, but the tightening of credit, Gross wrote.

He went on to prognosticate that interest rates
would have to come down to bring down mortgage
rates. He even presented a chart calculating the
amount that home prices or mortgage rates (or a
combination of the two) would have to decline to
revert back to previous affordability levels. "A forecast of home prices almost implicitly carries with
it a forecast for interest rates," he wrote, predicting
that, "The Fed will have to cut rates significantly
in coming years to stave off a double-digit decline
and reinvigorate the economy."

These coming rate cuts were nothing if not an opportunity for Pimco's clients, Gross wrote, opining that the subprime crisis wasn't all that bad. Investors, after all, he pointed out, could now look for "a bond bull market of still undefined proportions."

★★★★★

Predictably, backlash occurred. Bondholders were as much to blame as lenders, FDIC Chairman Sheila Bar said, according to the *Chicago Tribune* in April, 2007. "We should hold the servicers and the investors feet to the fire on this," Blair said angrily, testifying before the House Financial Services Committee. "We did not have good market discipline, with investors buying all these mortgages."

Indeed, bond investors *had* financed the housing boom with all those housing-backed securities—which replaced the traditional source for mortgage funds—banks. But those bond investors were starting to pay the price. According to Pimco, which was quoted in the *Tribune* article, those investors were losing as much as $75 billion on securities made up of millions of mortgages sold to people with poor credit. Some of the $450 billion in subprime mortgage-backed debt sold in 2006 had lost 37 percent in value, according to Merrill Lynch & Co.

Firms like Blackrock Inc., AllianceBernstein Holding LP, and Franklin Templeton Investments had
suddenly become vulnerable because of their zeal
to sell those mortgage bonds. About two-thirds of
mortgages got turned into bonds, way up from 40
percent in 1990, the year of the nation's last real
estate fiasco.

At that point in April, 2007, more than $6 trillion
of mortgage bonds was outstanding, the *Tribune*
noted, a sum that overshadowed the amount of
U.S. government debt by about 50 percent. "Bond
investors will be the ones who will take the losses,"
not the banks, said Pimco's Scott Simon.

Investors were losing money, Simon said, because
of places like Riverside County, Calif., where fore-
closures had almost tripled in the previous quarter
to 6,103 from a year earlier, the largest increase in
the U.S., according to Foreclosures.com.

Lehman Brothers Holdings Inc., the fourth-largest
U.S. securities firm, had used Riverside loans as
collateral for $1.5 billion of bonds sold in Janu-
ary, 2006. Some of the lowest-rated portions of the
securities were trading at 63 cents on the dollar,
down from more than 100 cents in October, according to data compiled by Merrill Lynch quoted
by the *Tribune*.

★★★★★

The result, as we all know now, was that Lehman tanked—but not before then-Treasury Secretary Hank Paulson and then-Federal Reserve Bank of New York President Timothy Geithner expended a lot of sweat equity trying to enable Barclays to acquire Lehman (a transaction nixed by British regulators, forcing Lehman into bankruptcy).

With support from the Fed, JPMorgan also acquired Bear Stearns and Bank of America Merrill Lynch. Credit markets went into lockdown. Companies outside of finance couldn't obtain financing or the funds they needed on a daily basis and the Dow dropped 30 percent. The global markets seemed poised for a complete meltdown. Paulson (who famously stated that the nation was just three days away from America's ATMs not working) et al. then proceeded to push for the famous (or infamous, depending on your view) $700 billion banking bailout from Congress in October ,2008.

Bill Gross again weighed in. In June, 2007, he had written in an "Investment Outlook" that "the flaw, dear readers," lay with the homes financed with cheap "and in some cases gratuitous money," as well as the ARM resets to come. He didn't dwell on exactly where that money originated.

In September, 2008 he was interviewed by the *Orange County Register* about the financial crisis, and this time defended Paulson's plan, then being debated in Congress, calling it an "investment" instead of a "bailout." Citizens should support the plan because "it will affect their jobs," Gross wrote. "It will affect unemployment. It will affect the state of the economy. Asset prices are deflating rapidly. Banks are unwilling to make loans. That means payrolls may even be suspended as the ability to lend money is curtailed. It really snowballs pretty quickly. . ."

The trick, Gross continued, was for the government to find the right price between the market value of the assets they were buying and the value they had on paper at the banks. As an example, Gross said his own firm recently had paid 65 cents on the dollar for a pool of mortgage-related assets. Loans and securities could trade from 20 cents on the dollar to 80 cents on the dollar, he said, but 65 cents was a good benchmark. In fact Pimco expected to earn a double-digit return on its money for the 65 cents on the dollar it paid.

The question before the government was finding the right price between 65 cents and 100 cents on the dollar, Gross explained. The closer the government got to 100 cents on the dollar, the better banks would like the deal. But the closer it stayed to 65 cents, the better the deal would be for taxpayers. Sixty-five cents on the dollar would be assuming that much as 30 percent of the loans being bought would end in foreclosure, and for every home that ends in foreclosure the investor would get as little as 40 cents on the dollar, Gross said.

★★★★★

Pimco itself, however, was feeling little pain from the financial crisis. At Gross's instigation, the Total Return Fund bought up bonds backed by income streams from Fannie Mae and Freddie Mac mortgage pools. The reasoning was that despite the housing crisis, the federal government would never let them fail. That reasoning was right. When the government took over Fannie and Freddie, the Pimco fund jumped 1.3 percent, its best day ever.

In 2008 Gross was named Morningstar Fixed-Income Fund Manager of the Year—for the third time—and the *Orange County Register* awarded him a victory lap: "It was roughly a year ago," the paper wrote in September, "that Gross took significant abuse for suggesting that the federal government provide broad financial support for the national housing market. Today, he looks darn bright about the need for federal aid."

Gross also heartily approved—in print—of the federal government's announcement that it was shoring up Fannie Mae and Freddie Mac to help lower mortgage rates. His support won Pimco recognition from faraway Washington: The firm was chosen that October to manage commercial paper assets for the Federal Reserve Bank as part of something called the Commercial Paper Funding Facility. That program would allow the government to backstop a market that corporations regularly use to fund their day-to-day operations. That market had been threatened during the financial meltdown.

The meltdown didn't seem to make a dent in Pimco & Co.'s ambitions to dominate as the Great Recession took center stage. El-Erian had returned the previous year after his short stint at Harvard (whose Harvard Fund, interestingly, rose 8.6 percent in the months after El-Erian's departure, in contrast with the S&P's 15 percent loss for the fiscal year ended June 30, 2008. The fund—absent El-Erian—then plunged 27.3 percent in FY '09).

El-Erian returned, rather triumphantly, to serve alongside Gross as Pimco's co-chief investment officer. In September, when longtime CEO Bill Thompson retired, El-Erian added "CEO" to his vita. Pimco at that point held $842 billion in assets under management, comprised of commodities, real estate, and passive equity.

El-Erian, the global markets expert, was implementing new ideas. One was the creation, in

October, 2008, of his own fund, the Global Asset Strategy Fund, as part of his aim to provide investors with more integrated products across asset classes, including equity. Indeed, as *Pensions & Investment* reported that October, Pimco planned to build an active equity management capability, possibly by lifting an existing team from a rival (a move Pimco would not comment on). "Pimco is moving toward providing investment thought relationship, as opposed to specifically fixed-income capabilities," a consultant, not identified, told the financial newspaper.

Central to that "thought relationship" was a term El-Erian coined, the "New Normal," referring to an investment environment that would likely not correct back to the bad old days but morph into something new—with more government involvement, slower growth, less risk-taking by investors, and lower consumer expectations. In short, his was a prediction of doom and gloom. "Unemployment is not only high, but it will remain high for a number of years," El-Erian later told Kiplinger.com. "Policy outcomes have consistently fallen short of expectations. This is not a classic recession. You have to deal with the debt overhang and the housing inventory." Despite all the uncertainties, El-Erian argued, "most people are still overexposed to risky assets."

Pimco itself had some setbacks. In February, 2009, *Fortune*'s respected financial writer, Allan Sloan, pointed out how Pimco, two months before, had been forced to postpone dividends on eight funds. Turns out the firm had used auction-rate preferred stock to borrow, but those auctions failed. It also made heavy bets on Treasury bond prices falling, but instead, those prices rose.

In all, however, Pimco seemed to be in great shape at the end of the decade. In the summer of 2009, it moved to grow its retail business by filing with the SEC to launch five active fixed-income exchange traded funds (ETFs), plus two more to track Treasury indices (Investopedia definition: an ETF is "a security that tracks an index, a commodity or a basket of assets like an index fund but trades like a stock on an exchange."). Over the previous year Pimco had launched 13 open-end mutual funds. Gross himself then took over primary responsibility for four closed-end funds.

Pimco Total Return, meanwhile, gained 4.8 percent that last year of the millenium's first decade, beating 90 percent of its peers, according to Morningstar. And Gross? To no one's surprise, he was named Fixed-Income Manager *of the Decade*.

Chapter 5

Recent Years

Cracks in the Crown

On January 21, 2014, shortly after Mohamed El-Erian announced his resignation, Bill Gross sent out a Twitter message to shore up investor confidence, expressing his own continuing fervor for the job. "PIMCO's fully engaged," he wrote. "Batteries 110% charged. I'm ready to go for another 40 years!"

But how many of those 40 years Pimco's chief would actually stick it out was anybody's guess. Gross after all was facing down his 70th birthday, on April 13. He also couldn't have had a presentiment of the firestorm about to erupt—specifically how the resignation of the much younger (55) El-Erian would prompt that *Wall Street Journal* article headlined "Inside the Showdown At the World's Biggest Bond Firm."

Beyond the tensions between the two men, 2013 had been a disastrous year for bond investors.

"Forget about the bond bloodbath in 1994," CNNMoney wrote in December of 2013. "This is shaping up to be the worst year in history for bond funds." Through the first week of that month, investors had pulled out an eye-popping $72 billion from bond mutual funds, according to TrimTabs data. "This is the first time in nearly a decade that investors have taken more money out of bond funds than they've put in," CNNMoney noted. Those withdrawals topped those of 1994, when investors withdrew almost $63 billion.

Blame the "taper talk" that had started back in May, 2014. Federal Reserve chief, Ben Bernanke began hinting that month that the central bank would begin to scale back its $85 billion a month in bond purchases. Those bond purchases had been aimed at keeping long-term interest rates low and stimulating the economy and the stock market.

So when would the tapering begin? Bond investors weren't waiting around to find out. After pouring money into bonds the first five months of 2013, they began a massive pullout, sending the Treasury bond yield from 1.6 percent in May to almost 3 percent by September. But the tapering didn't happen, and the yield crept back up to 2.5 percent; then the tapering talk resumed. Again, nothing happened, and the assumption came to be that Bernanke would leave the tapering to his successor,

Janet Yellen. (In reality the Fed started tapering in December and continued in April 2014.)

Pimco's Total Return Fund returns were down 1.9 percent in 2013—the fund's first down negative year since 1999—bringing the year's total outflows to a net $41.1 billion. That constituted more withdrawals in a year than for any fund in history, according to Morningstar.

"Clearly, Pimco's Bill Gross and the big bond boys are experiencing some performance issues," *Fortune* wrote. "The broader issue with bond managers like Pimco," the magazine posed, "is how far afield they have journeyed in search of yield. . . . At what cost does this hunt for yield come?"

What cost indeed? Bernanke said the government probably wouldn't raise interest rates until 2015. But Gross opined that ultra-low rates would stay in place, saying the economy wasn't ready for a rate hike. As for investors making guesses about the market, they should approach it, he wrote in his usual colorful, metaphor-heavy way, "like a totally hyena-aware lion cub—know there's bad things that can happen out there in the jungle, but for now enjoy the all clear silence of the African plain."

Bad things do happen, including to Pimco. By year's end, the Total Return Fund, which had become the world's largest mutual fund, in November, 2008, took a back seat to the Vanguard Total Stock Market Index Fund, which held $251 billion in assets—versus Total Return's (now diminished) $250 billion. Of course, back in 2008 investors had been pouring funds into bond funds as a safe harbor in the midst of the financial crisis. By late 2013, with tapering and an interest rate hike seemingly on the horizon, those same investors were now unloading bonds—with Treasurys having bottomed out three months in a row the previous summer, at 1.65 percent.

Gross, speaking and writing in various contexts, warned investors to get used to lower returns on stocks and bonds alike and to keep expectations low. "Neither Vanguard, PIMCO, Bridgewater, nor GMO, however, has discovered a cure for the common cold," he wrote in a December, 2013 "Investment Outlook." "Our performance periodically, and sometimes for frustrating long stretches, stuffs our noses or aches our heads, and makes us wonder why we hadn't been more careful about washing our hands during flu season."

★★★★★

Then came February and the *Wall Street Journal'* s world of hurt for Pimco public relations, with those allegations (backed by multiple sources) of tension at the firm as well as that now-infamous, profanity-laced confrontation between the managing director and El-Erian, his heir apparent.

Just the previous month, Douglas Hodge had been appointed CEO and Jay Jacobs, president, along with six deputy chief investment officers: Daniel Ivascyn, known for his mortgage-bond investment acumen; Andrew Balls, an expert on Europe; and Marc Seidner, set to take over some of El-Erian's global duties. Then Seider suddenly resigned, reportedly infuriating Gross. (The deputy list expanded to Mark Kiesel, Virginie Maisonneuve, Scott Mather and Mihir Worah.)

The new leadership, however, couldn't or wouldn't heal the hostile work environment which, according to *WSJ* reporting, involved a managing director (Gross) who did not welcome employees speaking with him or even making eye contact in the morning, scolded employees for actions as minor as not numbering the pages on presentations, and demanded that at least one portfolio manager who did not stand up for a client's visit write a $10,000 check to the charitable foundation (the poor guy complied and kept his job).

There was particular discord with El-Erian, though as recently as October the CEO had described Gross to *Fortune* as "really brilliant" and his own relationship with him as "a small complement, maybe 80/20. . . and I'm the '20' part."

By January, however, things had gone to hell. El-Erian agreed to work with a mediator. Gross nixed the idea. El-Erian announced his resignation and left the firm in March.

Gross moved quickly into damage-control mode. In a letter posted on the firm's website, he strongly praised the new administrative structure, writing, "We believe this new format, and the idea-sharing it will facilitate, will be more responsive to market developments. It will be great!"

He also gave press interviews. "All this discourse about an autocratic style from my standpoint and conflict between Mohammed and myself is over-blown," Gross said in a conversation with CNN's "Street Signs." He said that the autocratic style the *WSJ* had described was different from the shared responsibility of those six deputy CIOs. Those staffers also had been put on the investment committee at El-Erian's urging and with his full support, Gross said.

Asked about the allegations of enforced silence, reprimands, and no eye contact, Gross replied, "First of all I'm not a morning person...I have to get up at 4:30 in the morning. I'm better at 12 than I am at 7. He added later, "It takes four or five cups of coffee to wake up." Describing his own view of his relationship with El-Erian, Gross replied, "He's always been a good friend. His wife and my wife join together in terms of philanthropic activities. We see each other in town and at their home."

Gross's comments, however, failed to ameliorate Pimco's investors, who were blaming the firm's manager for misjudging the Federal Reserve's timing on scaling back its bond-buying program. In May, Deiter Wemmer, chief financial officer of the firm's parent, insurer Allianz, held a conference call with analysts. During that event, he called on Pimco to fix its problems, pointing out how investors had withdrawn a further $30 billion in the first quarter, which amounted to 11 straight months of withdrawals, and impacted group earnings. The withdrawals were split between the Total Return Fund and other fund families, Wemmer said.

What's more, investors were starting to come back to the bond market, "Just Not to PIMCO," according to the title of an April report compiled by Morningstar analyst Michael Rawson. The analyst wrote that investors had added $39 billion to long-term U.S. domiciled mutual funds in March, while Pimco continued to see net outflows over the same period.

El-Erian, who had a nondisclosure agreement with Pimco, stayed mostly mum on the subject of his departure, telling CNN in a longer interview about finance that he had felt it was time for him to do something different and that his leaving had been "a difficult personal decision." El-Erian, who retained a position with Allianz as chief economic advisor, was said to be writing a book on central banks.

In March, Morningstar issued a report expressing concerns that El-Erian's departure had raised "a higher degree of uncertainty" and that, absent El-Erian, the investment committee (which Morningstar said had the atmosphere of a "pressure cooker") now lacked a "senior statesmen" among its members, several of whom were "a bit less seasoned than their predecessors."

Headlines erupted when Morningstar downgraded Pimco's Stewardship Grade to Neutral while maintaining its Gold Rating for Pimco's Total Return Fund.

"PIMCO Total Return is still one of the best in class," Morningstar Russel Kimmel wrote. "We have highly rated funds from PIMCO in a wide array of bond categories, and that speaks to the depth of talent that is brought to bear at PIMCO Total Return. Bill Gross' name may be on the fund, but in fact, lots of people contribute to the fund's success. And, while Gross hasn't come off well in recent interviews, he's quite adept at bringing PIMCO's resources to bear for the fund's benefit."

Gross, meanwhile, was still second-guessing El-Erian's exit. In an April interview with Bloomberg, he seemed to challenge El-Erian to reveal why he'd left. Recalling his own dialogue with his number-two, Gross said, "He simply said he was not the man to take the company forward."

Gross also described his own response to El-Erian's announcement: "I would say, 'Come on, Mohamed, tell us why,' " but, Gross insisted, he got no satisfactory answer.

Gross added that he'd asked himself in recent months whether the depictions of him were true. He said he'd concluded they were not and that, in any case, he was trying to change. "I look in the mirror, you know, and I like my hair. It's nice and thick," Gross said. "But can it be changed, can it be a different style, can it be trimmed at a certain level? Of course it can, and that's what I'm trying to do."

★★★★★

Pimco wasn't out of the woods by any measure. In April, *Bloomberg Businessweek* reported that the firm's Pimco Unconstrained Bond Fund—designed to make money even if interest rates rose—had lost $2.7 billion to redemptions while similar funds at Goldman Sachs, JP Morgan Chase, and Black Rock had actually seen a "surge" of deposits. "Pimco has kind of shot themselves in the foot here," Steve Roge, a money manager with R.W. Roge & Co., told the magazine. "In a new category where there are other choices, why is someone going to look at a fund that has been a bottom performer?"

Indeed, in March, the JPMorgan Strategic Income Opportunities Fund overtook Pimco in the non-traditional bond fund category. Another possible reason for Pimco's lag: The Unconstrained Bond Fund's manager, Chris Dialynas, had been on sabbatical since December, after running the fund since its creation in 2008. Gross took over management of the fund, a move that underlined its importance. Gross also extended the fund's duration, or sensitivity to interest rates.

But the magic was gone. In April, Morningstar dropped the Unconstrained Fund's rating from bronze to neutral. It was behind 55 percent of similar funds and had lost $2.7 billion in redemptions through March, Morningstar said.

According to the *Bloomberg Businessweek* story, the Unconstrained Fund had been hurt in 2013 because it held intermediate- and long-dated bonds at a time when then-Fed Chairman Bernanke "hinted" that the central bank might scale back its bond-buying program. The subsequent increase in interest rates caused those bonds to lose value.

The magazine kept up the pressure on Gross, making him the subject of an April 10 cover story whose cover photo depicted the managing director looking directly at the camera with his palms upraised. The headline read, "Am I Really Such a Jerk?"

Gross was interviewed for the article, in which he told reporter Sheelah Kolhatkar, "It's been like a near-death experience, an emotional blow. Whenever I read the newspaper, I say to myself, 'At least my wife loves me.'"

The piece was informative for its description of Gross's life, both in general and post-El-Erian specifically. "He collects a Starbucks black eye ('it's got two shots of whatever they shoot it with'), makes his way to his U-shaped desk in the center of Pimco's trading floor, and activates his seven monitors: 7- and 10-year Treasury futures; sovereign credit-default swap spreads; corporate bonds; stocks; cash Treasury bonds; and e-mail," Kolhatkar wrote of the Pimco chief's routine each morning after rising at 4:30 a.m.

Gross then reviews a printout of the $470 billion worth of portfolios he personally oversees, the article continued. Employees arrive, ahead of the 6:30 a.m. (Pacific Time) opening of the stock market. "Also, the spot on the trading floor where El-Erian's desk once sat is now empty, and staffers avoid it," Kolhatkar wrote, injecting a dash of black humor. "One gets the sense that people go out of their way to walk around it, as if avoiding the chalk outline of a murder victim on the sidewalk."

The article went on to examine more deeply than other media had, the psychological factors motivating El-Erian's unhappy departure. "Because of his personality, Mohamed was able to do a lot of managing of people in ways that Bill didn't want to, and to this day probably doesn't care to," Morningstar senior analyst Eric Jacobson told the magazine. Conflict had likely sprung, Jacobson said, from El-Erian's management of the Global Multi-Asset Fund, which had suffered an 8 percent loss in 2013 and compared poorly with comparable funds.

Meanwhile, at Allianz, some of the insurer's largest shareholders were lobbying for the parent company to increase its oversight of Pimco and—unusual in Germany—to go public with news of that oversight at the next shareholder meeting in May. Several, quoted anonymously by Reuters, said they wanted Allianz specifically to rethink the new management structure and Gross's pay (reportedly $200 million a year). "The leash is obviously too long because there is a performance issue now," said one top-10 investor. "A fully owned subsidiary should not be run like this."

★★★★★

As expected, those leading investors complained bitterly about Pimco at the insurer's May 7 shareholders meeting in Munich. "Pimco's halo is crumbling, and with it Allianz's share price," said Union investment portfolio manager, Ingo Speich. But Allianz's chief executive, Michael Diekmann, disagreed.

Diekmann, according to a report from Reuters, said that investors needed to ignore short-term volatility. Pimco, he said, had produced better returns than many of its competitors for most of the past 25 years. "There is really no reason to rake us over the coals or to sense the end is at hand," Diekmann said, noting that Pimco's customers had actually largely supported the new team of six deputy chief investment officers backing up Gross since El-Erian's departure. "Responsibilities within Pimco have been redistributed and clearly regulated," Diekmann said. "They now lie on more shoulders."

"Allianz will do anything sensible to strengthen Pimco further," he added. "Clients gave us a very positive feedback regarding Pimco's new management structure."

A lot was at stake for Allianz, considering that over the previous decade Pimco had contributed to the German group's operating profit an amount that had climbed fourfold to $4.46 billion (3.2 billion euros), representing a third of total core earnings. Perhaps because of this history, despite Pimco's failings and administrative shake-up, the insurer made it clear it was sticking by its cash cow.

★★★★★

Some things began looking up for Pimco in late April. First, El-Erian—who had begun writing a column for Bloomberg, contributed commentary to *Financial Times,* and was a member of President Barack Obama's Global Economic Development Council—generously praised his former boss at Pimco (without commenting on their personal relationship).

"I have had the privilege of watching him in action and he is just a great investor," El-Erian said in an interview with Bloomberg Television. "Bill is one of the world's best investors . . . . He's able to differentiate signals from noise and is committed to delivering value."

Pimco meanwhile counseled investors, in a May 13 secular outlook, that a mantra called the "New Neutral" was supplanting the New Normal. The managers who wrote the report said they now saw a global economy weighted down under debt, including a "sharp increase" in China's debt, and an economy that couldn't generate demand sufficient to keep up with potential output. "In the absence of a new growth model," the *WSJ* reported of Pimco's modified stance, "the reality in most developed economies—and even some developing economies—is going to be a world of essentially 0% real interest rates."

Neutral real, or inflation-adjusted, central bank policy interest rates close to zero suggest "an end to Bull Markets as we have known them, but no perceptible growling from the Bears," LiveTrading-News.com wrote of the Pimco report, noting that the firm saw perhaps 3 percent returns for bonds and 5 percent for stocks over the next three to five years.

The upshot? Nations would converge toward modest potential growth rates: 1 percent for Europe's GDP and 6 percent to 6.5 percent for China, with better growth prospects for the United States.

Meanwhile, back at "The Beach," Pimco, in late May announced it had rehired Paul McCulley, a former senior executive at the firm, to fill the new job of chief economist and to join the Investment Committee. "We thought that Paul would be the unifying force, so to speak, of the firm's new structure, which includes six deputy chief investment officers," Gross said of McCulley's return.

That event couldn't come too soon, seeing as how investors had withdrawn $55 billion from the $230 billion Total Return Fund over the previous year.

McCulley, the *WSJ* noted, would be working only about 100 days a year while also becoming something of a public face (to replace Gross? observers had to wonder), writing research papers, and appearing on television. McCulley already had worked two stints at Pimco but had left to take up philanthropy and angel investing.

Now he was back, and the response was positive. "It soothes the fear that Pimco is losing its way after the departure of Mohamed El-Erian," Jeff Tjornehoj, head of Lipper Americas Research, told the *Journal*.

Finally, there seemed to be lght at the end of the tunnel regarding all those outflows: $3.1 billion in net outflows in April, its 12th month in a row of redemptions, according to Morningstar Inc. "We are already seeing a revival in demand for bonds," Pimco Chief Executive Hodge told the German newspaper *Boersen-Zeitung*. "That is evident in both the decline of the yield levels and in the money flows into our fund."

★★★★★

These factors in May, 2014 predicted "slower yet increasingly stable growth rates," Gross wrote, describing a scenario with more risk than reward. "Financial repression as it continues for years to come will almost ensure that outcome," Gross wrote. Investors might hope for rates of 1 percent to 2 percent, but Gross saw them remaining closer to 0 percent.

"If the future resembles those neutral policy rates, then the investment implications are striking: low returns yet less downside risk than investors currently expect; an end to bull markets as we've known them, but no perceptible growling from the bears," Gross concluded. And investors listened.

While the managing director of Pimco had had his missteps in the previous years, his words still made headlines. After all, he was, and is, the Bond King, sitting atop the world's largest bond fund.

Chapter 6

Current Events

Pimco Without Bill Gross

On Friday. September 26, 2014 at 5:30 a.m., after spending a half hour in his office, Bill Gross resigned from Pimco. Pimco's co-founder and chief investment officer left before Pimco's board, which was poised to fire him, could announce their intent. He left without severance to join the Janus Capital Group, Inc. At Janus, the man who built Pimco into a $2 trillion gorilla, was to manage a $13 million Janus fund from a new office in Newport Beach California.

The Pimco board could no longer tolerate Gross's eccentric personality and rather erratic management style. Senior managers had threatened the board with their resignation if something were not done about Bill Gross. Aware of the board's displeasure and intent to fire him, Gross announced his resignation.

According to the Wall Street Journal, "As Pimco executives struggled to process the news, phone lines chirped with confused clients. Competitors formulated strategies to steal Pimco's longtime investors. Tens of billions, if not hundreds of billions of dollars were at stake.

Bond investors tend to be very loyal to a particular fund manager and the movement of a manager generates industry ripples. The movement of the world's most prominent fund manager set waves in motion throughout the $38 trillion bond market.

In less than a week, investors pulled a net $23.5 billion from Bill Gross's Total Return fund at Pimco. During the dramatic last week of September, 2014 only $66.4 million was newly invested with Bill Gross's new Janus fund. The small fund closed September with a $79.1 million portfolio.

Pimco CEO, Douglas Hodge, said he was confident that that the vast majority of Pimco customers would remain loyal. Pimco certainly retained an impressive list of fund managers and executives.

Morning Star, Inc. calculates that fourteen cents of each dollar in taxable funds is vested in Pimco funds according to the Wall Street Journal. Additionally, the Journal reports that 28,000 401k retirement plans have $88 billion invested with the Total Return fund, according to BrightScope, a retirement research firm.

After 40 years at Pimco, at the age of 70, Bill Gross left feeling vengeful according to some.

The public displays of difficulties at Pimco appeared in January of 2014 when Mohamed El-Erian, Gross's apparent successor, abruptly quit.

Bill Gross earned $200 million at Pimco during 2013. He went to Janus without negotiating a salary.

Pimco has experienced outflows as a result of Gross's departure, but it is staffed with talent. Fund managers and traders are paid great sums if they can anticipate fluctuations and trends. That talent is a not a monopoly possessed by one man or woman, it is distributed to many in varied degrees. Pimco's potential for future success lies with the excellence of its executives and fund managers. The departure of Bill Gross is not catastrophic, it is merely a chapter in Pimco's history.

www.ingramcontent.com/pod-product-compliance
Lightning Source LLC
Chambersburg PA
CBHW060621200326
41521CB00007B/840